ISLAM AND THE BIBLE

The Bible the Qur'an Affirms is the very Bible it Denies

BY KEIRON LONG

Islam and the Bible:
The Bible the Qur'an Affirms is the very Bible it Denies
By Keiron Long
Contact: keironlong@pm.me
© Copyright 2025. All right reserved.
ISBN 978-1-7642784-0-9

Cover:	Rainbow over Meteora, Greece. Photo by Keiron Long
Back cover:	The bones of the Otranto martyrs in a side chapel of Otranto Cathedral. Photo by Keiron Long.
Images:	Wikimedia Commons and Keiron Long.
Design:	South Star Design

Contents

FOREWORD — 3

CHAPTER 1: INTRODUCTION — 4
- Muhammed — 7
- Islam's Expansion and the Ishmaelite Claim — 9
- Muhammad's Early Challenges — 10
- Power Struggles and Consolidation in Arabia — 11
- Military Expansion and Religious Supremacy — 12
- The Geopolitical View — 13
- The Death of Muhammad — 16
- Persecution and the Christian Response — 21

CHAPTER 2: THE BIBLE — 24
- Why do Muslims avoid reading the Bible — 24
- The Origins of the corruption thesis — 25
- Overlooked Qur'anic Affirmations — 27
- Did Ibn Abbas Believe the Bible Was Textually Corrupted? — 28
- The Mawali and Early Islamic Engagement with the Bible — 29
- Ibn Hazm and the Doctrine of Tahrif — 31
- Manuscript Evidence and Biblical Stability — 32
- Revelation and the Canon — 33
- Trapped by Their Own Reasoning: Qur'anic Contradictions — 33
- Isaac or Ishmael: Who was the child of sacrifice? — 35
- Pentecost and the Holy Spirit — 38
- The Role of Gabriel in Scripture — 39
- The True Meaning of Pentecost — 39
- The Descent of the Holy Spirit — 40
- No Connection to Muhammad — 41
- The nature of Jesus: divine or merely a prophet — 42
- The Qur'an's Accusation Against Christianity — 43
- Jesus Testifies to His Own Divinity — 45
- The Council of Nicaea — 47
- Mary: The God-bearer (Theotokos) or righteous woman? — 51
- The Council of Ephesus and the Theotokos — 53
- The Role of the Bishop of Rome — 54
- The Council of Ephesus — 55
- The Crucifixion — 56
- Why Would Islam Deny the Cross? — 58
- The Nature of Salvation: Christianity vs. Islam — 61
- Grace and the Sacraments — 63
- The Roots of the Islamic Tradition — 66
- The Biblical Account — 67

Marriage: Sacramental covenant or dissolvable contract?	70
Marriage in Heaven	72
The Divine Order of Marriage	73
Jihad: Spiritual struggle or holy war?	75
The Military Struggle	76
Comparison with Israelite and Christian Scriptures	77
The Figurative Use of "Sword" in Christianity	79
Conclusion	80

CHAPTER 3: FAULT LINES OF FAITH — 81

The Spread of Islam	81
Islam Moves into France	83
First Constantinople, Then Rome	85
The Knights of Malta	88
Islam's Advance into Europe and Beyond	88
The Greek Struggle for Independence	89
Clash of Faiths	90
Sunni versus Shia	92
Islam and Culture	95
Arius and the Trinity	97
Messengers from Heaven	101
Why Fatima? A Historical and Spiritual Connection	101
The Apparitions of Fatima	103
Messages and Warnings from Heaven	103
Prophecies of War and Persecution	104
Mary's Five Sorrows	105
Other Apparitions Throughout History	105
Icons	107
A Venerable Icon	108
Saint John of Damascus and the Veneration of Icons	108
Conclusion	110
Apologia by St John of Damascus (The Defence of Icons)	111

REFLECTIONS — 130

NOTES — 133

The Rosary	133
"If anyone thirsts, let him come to Me." (John 7:37)	133
Tradition: Word of Mouth and in Writing	134
Suicide	134

PICTURES — 136
MAPS — 136
REFERENCES — 137
BIBLIOGRAPHY — 137

Foreword

My earlier Booklet, *Muhammed and the twelve Tribes of Ishmael*, (2022) used a simple analogy comparing the Trinity with water (water, steam or ice). This was included along with Aquinas's definition of the Trinity. However, a philosopher acquaintance told me that the water analogy wasn't theologically sound as it fell under a heresy called Modalism. Not wanting to use a leaky analogy I resolved to revise my booklet and use the opportunity to include new knowledge, questions and to think of a new title, namely, *Islam and the Bible: The Bible the Qur'an Affirms is the very Bible it Denies*.

On completing the final draft of this booklet, I sent it to a friend who kindly read over it and provided some helpful feedback. My next step was to use GPT-Chat as an editorial tool to help refine it further. I then asked GPT-Chat to kindly provide an acknowledgement, which follows below:

"I would like to express my gratitude to GPT-Chat, an AI language model developed by OpenAI, for its assistance in refining the clarity, structure, and flow of this work. While every perspective and conclusion in these pages is my own, GPT-Chat provided valuable help in organizing material, sharpening historical references, and suggesting ways to make the presentation more engaging for readers.

Its contributions have been a tool in service of the message I wish to communicate, the enduring truth of God's covenant as revealed in Scripture."

Amen! to that.

> *"A thousand years in your sight are like a day that has just gone by, or like a watch in the night."*
>
> (PSALM 90:4)

CHAPTER 1: INTRODUCTION

As history unfolds, like a day that has just gone by, empires rise and fall. The Persians, Greeks, and Romans each occupy the land of Israel. The Romans come like a watch in the night, heralding the birth of Jesus in the town of Bethlehem, in the province of Judea.

His disciples declare Jesus to be the Mashiach, The Messiah, or Christos in Greek, the Anointed One. His followers believe that God's covenant with Abraham reaches its fulfillment in Jesus, for as the prophet Micah had foretold:

"And thou, Bethlehem Ephrata, art a little one among the thousands of Judah: out of thee shall he come forth unto me that is to be ruler in Israel: and his going forth is from *the beginning, from the days of eternity.*" (Micah 5:2)

And didn't Isaiah proclaim:

"For a child is born to us… and His name shall be called Wonderful, Counsellor, *God the Almighty, the Father of the world to come.*" (Isaiah 9:6)

The prophets are proclaiming that God Himself will enter history. And it is through the House of Judah that God chooses to fulfil the words of the prophets.

Jesus is born into the House of Judah, a tribe descending from Abraham through his son Isaac, the son God miraculously promised to Sarah.

The story of Isaac is about a son of promise, one given by divine intervention. God tells Abraham that it will be through Sarah, his barren wife, that the covenant will be established.

"Your wife Sarah will bear you a son, and you will call him Isaac. I will establish my covenant with him as an everlasting covenant for his descendants after him." (Genesis 17:19).

Isaac's older half-brother Ishmael was also blessed by God, but Isaac was promised. This distinction becomes the dividing line between an inheritance according to the flesh and an inheritance by a promise, The covenant flows not through the eldest son, but through the promised one, a pattern that continues from Isaac to Jacob, from David to Christ.

The covenant continues in an unexpected way when Isaac's son Jacob, not the elder brother Esau, receives the blessing. After wrestling with God (Genesis 32), Jacob's name is changed to Israel; the one who struggles with God and prevails through perseverance. From his line come the twelve tribes of Israel, the very foundation stones of the people of the covenant.

From among those twelve tribes, the tribe of Judah is chosen to bring the promise forward. And from the House of Judah comes David, the youngest of eight brothers. While hereditary honours the firstborn, God chooses by looking into the heart. God chose David and he was anointed king.

The prophet Nathan tells David:

"I will raise up your offspring after you… and I will establish the throne of his kingdom forever." (2 Sam 7:12-13)

Then, when the long-awaited heir to David's throne comes to reign over the Kingdom of Heaven He is testified to by His Companions.

"The book of the genealogy of Jesus Christ, the son of David, the son of Abraham…" (Matt 1:1)

And so the promise flows from Abraham to Isaac, from Isaac to Jacob (Israel), from Jacob to Judah, from Judah to David and finally to Jesus, who is called Son of David. Yet, his kingdom is not of this world because it is a kingdom of Faith.

Muhammed

Six centuries after Jesus is born in Bethlehem, a man named Muhammad (570 – 632) emerges from the deserts of Arabia, claiming to be receiving divine revelations from the angel Gabriel, or Jibril in Arabic. He will reshape the world through preaching and through conquest, all in the name of Allah (God).

Muhammad belongs to the Quraysh, a prominent Meccan tribe. The Quraysh trace their lineage to Adnan, whom they believe descends from Ishmael, Abraham's son by Hagar who was Sarah's Egyptian maidservant.

Though many among the Quraysh elite reject his message, Muhammad gradually gathers followers. What began as a lone voice soon becomes a growing movement. When he is forced to flee his native Mecca Muhammad travels north-west to Medina (Yathrib), some 450 kilometres away. There, he becomes not only a self-proclaimed prophet, but a political leader and military commander. By the time of his death, he has united much of Arabia under the banner of a new faith.

His followers name this new faith Islam, meaning submission. Those who embrace it are called Muslims, those who submit. Submission to God, they say, requires Jihad, an internal struggle for righteousness and, when necessary, a military struggle to defend God's messenger and his book.

Islam presents itself as both a revelation and a restoration. It was, they believe, the final and perfect message from God, delivered in a pure form, uncorrupted. But it also wanted to establish a new truth. While Jews and Christians held to the line of Isaac, Muslims insist that Ishmael, the elder son, had been wrongly cast aside. God had now chosen his last and greatest messenger from the line of Ishmael, and the chosen messenger was Muhammed. Some of Muhammed's followers even claim the Scriptures have been altered to favour Isaac, reasoning that as the firstborn, Ishmael was the rightful heir of Abraham's promise.

For Christians this claim represents a rejection of Scripture because they believe the covenant is fulfilled through Isaac's line and culminates in Jesus Christ, to whom the prophets Micah and Isaiah spoke of as the true fulfillment of God's promise to Abraham. To say the covenant passes instead through Ishmael to Muhammad is a contradiction. The promise has been realized in Christ, "the image of the unseen God and the first born of creation." (Col. 1:15) It was not a promise still awaiting completion or a new beginning.

However, the Ishmaelites reject Christ (The Anointed One) as coming from "the days of eternity" and turn to one of their own, Muhammad, accepting his new interpretation of Abraham's legacy.

And with Muhammad's conquests, the claim that God has chosen someone from the line of Ishmael began to spread, not only by persuasion, but by power.

Islam's Expansion and the Ishmaelite Claim

The inheritance of Abraham became the battleground of empires. While Christians believe in a spiritual kingdom based on a covenant through Isaac, the followers of Muhammad seize land, cities, and sanctuaries in Ishmael's name.

In *Slaves on Horseback* historian Patricia Crone observes that "Islamic civilization is the only one in the world to begin in the mind of a single man." and that Muhammad "predisposed the Arabs for conquest on the model of the Jews."[1] But where the Israelites (Jews) were given boundaries by divine command, Muhammad imposed no limits.

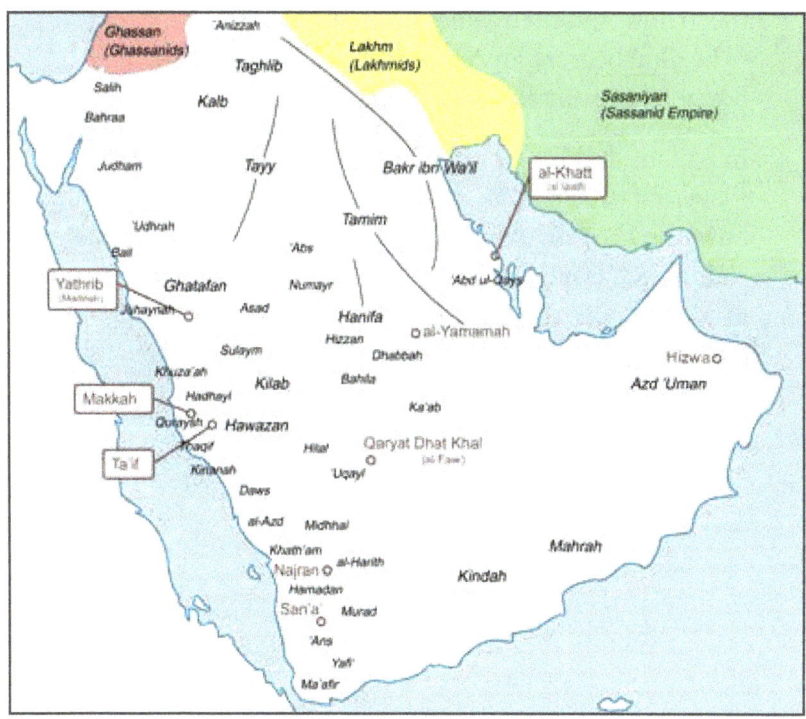

Arabia in the time of Muhammed / Wikimedia Commons.

Muhammad's Early Challenges

The earliest surviving biography glorifying Muhammad as God's final messenger is attributed to Ibn (son of) Hisham (d. 833), who preserved and edited the earlier work of Ibn Ishaq (Isaac. d. 767). This text presents Muhammad as a prophet not merely for Arabia, but for all nations.

According to Ibn Hisham, Muhammad initially coexisted peacefully in Mecca's multi-faith society. However, when he began preaching strict monotheism, declaring that "God has no associates," he faced increasing hostility. Eventually, he and his followers sought refuge elsewhere. The southern Christian town of Najran was not an option, as Muhammad regarded Christians as polytheists for their belief in the Trinity and their veneration of Mary as Theotokos (The God bearer). Instead, he turned north to Medina, home to a strong Jewish community.

In 622, he and his Companions undertook the Hijra (Severing of Relations), a break not only from Mecca, but from the religious frameworks that had rejected his claims. Yet, even as Muhammad forged a new community in Medina, divisions loomed. His cousin Ali and his chief adviser Abu Bakr would later clash over succession, marking the beginning of internal division even as Islam's external strength grew.

Power Struggles and Consolidation in Arabia

Upon arriving in Medina, Muhammad and his followers were quickly accepted by the city's leaders, forming a new power bloc alongside a number of Jewish clans. Meanwhile, the other dominant Arab confederacies, the Ghassanids in the north, aligned with the Eastern Roman Empire, and the Lakhmids in the northeast, aligned with the Persian Sassanid Empire, continued to wield power and influence.

Tensions soon arose between Muhammad and the Jewish clans. According to Ibn Hisham he instructed his followers to pray facing Jerusalem, likely in the hope of gaining Israelite support. A document known as the Constitution of Medina (622), called for unity among the city's various clans, including Jewish ones. Yet, while it lists several minor Jewish groups, it leaves out the three largest Jewish clans, all of whom would later come into conflict with Muhammad. The Constitution is often described as a defensive pact but Muhammad's actions were hardly defensive, nor did they reflect the spirit of unity the document claims to promote. In addition, from the perspective of the Jewish clans, even the minor ones, aligning themselves with Muhammad would have meant transgressing some of Moses's commandments, particularly the prohibition against coveting a neighbour's property. This moral question alone suggests the Constitution's validity is somewhat questionable. Joseph Spoerl writes in, *Muhammad and the Jews according to Ibn Ishaq*,[2] that Muhammad's attitude toward the Israelites hardened over time because according to Ibn Ishaq, "The Jewish Rabbis used to annoy the apostle with questions and introduce confusion, so as to confound the truth with falsity." Unable to persuade them that a prophet has come from the line of Ishmael, Ibn Ishaq says Muhammad ultimately attributed their rejection to envy and obstinacy.

Military Expansion and Religious Supremacy

Victory at the Battle of Badr in 624 marked a turning point because Muhammad now wielded both religious and military authority. He warned the Israelite tribe of Banu Qaynuqa:

"O Jews, beware lest God bring upon you the vengeance that He brought upon the Quraysh. Become Muslims. You know that I am a prophet who has been sent—you will find that in your scriptures and in God's covenant with you."

The Jewish leaders denied any such covenant or prophetic reference and because of their resistance the Banu Qaynuqa were expelled and their property seized. The pattern continued with the Banu Nadir who were expelled in 625. Then the Banu Qurayza met a tragic fate in 627. After being accused of political disloyalty during the Battle of the Trench, and some other minor crimes, the men were executed and their families enslaved.

These were not isolated incidents; they marked the systematic removal of those who rejected Muhammad's religious and political authority.

From Medina, Muhammad rapidly consolidated power across Arabia. Ibn Hisham presents these conquests not merely as political events but as divine campaigns; holy wars against those who denied Muhammad's mission and gave God associates.

Modern Muslim historians often echo Ibn Hisham, portraying Arab expansion as a crusade for the oneness of God (tawhid) and a vindication of Ishmael's line over that of Isaac. Other Muslim historians such as Philip Hitti, in *History of the Arabs*, concede that economic motives existed:

"The clerical interpretation of the Islamic movement emphasised in Arabic sources makes it entirely or primarily a religious movement and lays no emphasis, no stress on the underlying economic causes."[3]

Yet, Hitti does not hesitate to portray Islam as a militant religious movement, as shown by his commentary on the 630 attack on the village of Mu'tah in Jordan. In his account of the event, Hitti writes:

"The event was naturally interpreted as one of the ordinary raids…. but actually, it was the first gun in a struggle that was not to cease until the proud Byzantine capital had fallen to the latest champions of Islam and the name of Muhammad substituted for that of Christ on the walls of the most magnificent cathedral of Christendom, St. Sofia."[4]

While Muslim historians emphasize Muhammad's divine mission, secular historians tend to argue that the rise of Arab power had more to do with politics, economics, and the strategic collapse of surrounding empires.

The Geopolitical View

Those historians who do not regard Arab expansionism as primarily driven by religious zeal emphasize the influence of broader geopolitical forces shaping the Middle East at the time. They view religion as a secondary factor in the rise of the Arab confederacy. Supporters of this perspective point to the declining power of the dominant empires of the day.

In his book, *In God's Path*, Robert G. Hoyland summarizes this perspective:

"The Arab conquests began as an Arab insurrection—that is, the early conquests were not invaders coming from outside the empire but insiders trying to seize a share of the power and wealth of the Byzantine state."[5]

Byzantium, or the Eastern Roman Empire, was established in 286 when Emperor Diocletian divided Rome into eastern and western halves to improve administrative governance. Its capital, Constantinople (now Istanbul), was built by Constantine, the empire's first Christian ruler.

During Muhammad's lifetime, the Persian (Sassanid) and Byzantine empires were locked in a costly war (602–628). Both emerged severely weakened, creating a power vacuum in the Middle East. In addition to the political instability there were climatic disruptions caused by volcanic eruptions (c. 536 - 660), leading to crop failures across Europe and the Middle East. Plagues devastated urban populations, and disbanded mercenaries, struggling to find employment, were easily drawn to Muhammad's cause. Heavy taxation to fund the wars further eroded public support for the ruling powers. Additionally, religious divisions within Christianity lessened support for imperial authority, especially the Christian Schisms in Syria, Egypt, Iraq, and Persia which bred resentment toward the emperors in Constantinople.[6]

Given all of these events the tide was right for the Arabs and they needed to take it at the flood, or see the destiny of their voyage bound in the shallows and miseries of receding empires. Muhammed's Medina confederacy took the tide, surfed a wave of good fortune, and in a series of swift manoeuvres claimed much of the territory formally held by the two declining super powers.

However, while modern historians increasingly attribute Arab imperialism to economic instability, military disarray, antagonism between Arians and orthodox Christians and Jewish communities, in addition to tribal opportunism, Islamic historians downplayed these factors. For them, the story was not one of strategic timing, but divine providence. Arab conquests were written into Muslim history as the will of God, carried out by His final and greatest messenger, Muhammad.

Byzantine and Sassanid Empires in 600 AD / Wikimedia Commons.

The Death of Muhammad

The death of Muhammad in 632 marked a turning point in Islamic history, as tribal elders selected Abu Bakr as the new leader. His appointment led to several lasting consequences.

Firstly, it resulted in the division of Islam into two major factions: Sunni and Shiite. Ali, Muhammad's cousin and husband of his favourite daughter, Fatima, was supported by those who believed that leadership should remain within Muhammad's family. However, Abu Bakr's selection as Caliph (Successor) marked the beginning of Sunni dominance, leading to Ali and his followers gradually forming the Shiite faction, a split that continues to this day.

Additionally, Abu Bakr's leadership created a caliphate of political and religious authority, raising questions about whether the most powerful political leader should also claim religious leadership. Christianity faced a similar struggle, particularly in Byzantium, where Eastern Roman emperors often sought to wield both secular and religious power.

Once elected, Abu Bakr continued the expansionist policies inspired by Muhammed. Ibn Ishaq quotes Abu Bakr as saying:

"God sent Muhammad with his religion and strove for it until men accepted it voluntarily or by force."

In 633, he dispatched military expeditions northward into the Ghassan territories around Jordan and Syria. After capturing Damascus in 634, the Medina confederacy established it as their new capital. Upon Abu Bakr's death in 634, Umar succeeded him as Caliph and set his sights on Jerusalem. His task was made easier by the Byzantines' defeat at the Battle of Yarmouk in 636, weakening their hold on the region. Many Ghassan Arabs, former Byzantine allies, either joined the Medina confederacy or sought refuge in Lebanon to preserve their culture and Christian identity.

In 637, Umar's forces advanced on Jerusalem and a sermon by Sophronius, the Patriarch at the time, paints a gloomy picture:

"Why are the troops of the Saracens attacking us? Why has there been so much destruction and plunder? Why are there incessant outpourings of human blood? Why are the birds of the sky devouring human bodies? Why have churches been pulled down? Why is the cross mocked? Why is Christ, who is the dispenser of all good things and the provider of this joyousness of ours, blasphemed by pagan mouths so that he justly cries out to us: 'Because of you my name is blasphemed among the pagans,' and this is the worst of all the terrible things that are happening to us." (Sermon, December 6, 636/7)

After securing Jerusalem, Umar ordered the construction of a prayer site for Muslims on the Temple Mount. This first mosque, a wooden structure, at a place known as Al-Haram al-Sharif (the Noble Sanctuary), served as the primary place of worship for over fifty years until the rise of the Umayyad Dynasty in 661. In his article, *The Muslim Claim to Jerusalem*[7], Daniel Pipes suggests Jerusalem's historical significance to the Umayyad's was fundamentally political, but given the Caliph was a political and religion authority, religion was the stage on which the political drama unfolded.

Once the Umayyad's controlled Jerusalem they strategically sought to elevate the city's religious significance, positioning it as a rival to Mecca; probably because the Ali faction (Shiite) was still strong in Mecca and Medina, especially during the time of Husayn ibn Ali and Abdullah ibn az-Zubayr, both of whom rejected the legitimacy of Umayyad rule and frowned upon Islamic power being centralised in the Syrian capital of Damascus. Husayn ibn Ali was the son of Fatima and Ali, while Abdullah ibn az-Zubayr was the son of Asma, the daughter of Abu Bakr, the first Caliph. After the Umayyad's solidified their power by defeating the Ali faction in a number of battles, they continued building their power base in Damascus and promoting Jerusalem over Mecca. In 688-691 Caliph Abd al-Malik ibn Marwan built a grand shrine known as the Dome of the Rock. Then, under al-Walid the First a new mosque was built in about 705 and given the name Al-Aqsa Mosque (the Farthest Mosque).

To further strengthen their religious legitimacy the Umayyads promoted the interpretation that a night journey attributed to Muhammad was a miraculous visit to Jerusalem. Yet, no mosque existed on the Temple Mount during his lifetime because Caliph Umar built Jerusalem's first Mosque, the Al-Haram al-Sharif Mosque around 637, five years after Muhammad's death, and the Roman General Titus had destroyed the Jewish Temple in the year 70 as retribution for an Israelite rebellion.

The relevant Quranic verse recording a night journey states:

"Glory to (Allah) Who did take His Servant for a Journey by night from the Sacred Mosque to the Farthest Mosque (Masjid al-Aqsa), whose precincts We did bless, in order that We might show him some of Our Signs: for He is the One Who heareth and seeth (all things)." (Qur'an 17:1)

Notably, the Quran does not mention Muhammad by name in this passage. The Umayyads named their mosque Masjid al-Aqsa (the Farthest Mosque), effectively embedding their interpretation into Islamic tradition.

However, alternative explanations exist for the location of the Farthest Mosque. Masjid al-Aqsa may refer to a sacred site near Mecca, such as Al-Mashar Al-Haram, where Muhammad prayed during his farewell pilgrimage to Mount Arafat, some twenty kilometres southeast of Mecca. Al-Mash'ar al-Haram is approximately seven to nine kilometres from the centre of Mecca, a journey often made at night to avoid the heat of the day.

Others ask if the Night Journey refers to the angel Gabriel as described in the Book of Daniel. This intriguing hypothesis suggests the night journey refers to the angel Gabriel's visit to the servant of God, Daniel: 9:21

"While I was still praying, Gabriel, the man I had seen in the earlier vision, came to me in swift flight about the time of the evening prayer."

God sent Gabriel on this night flight to give Daniel, "skill and understanding" and to "seal up the vision and prophecy, and to anoint the most Holy." Christians interpret this as a prediction about the Christos, who was to come after seven weeks and sixty-two weeks of years, and who would be slain and denied by many. Afterward, "a people with their leader... shall destroy the city and the sanctuary," as Titus did in 70 AD.

The Prophet Daniel also foretold the coming of one like the Son of Man:

"I saw in the night visions, and behold, with the clouds of heaven there came one like a son of man, and he came to the Ancient of Days and was presented before him. And to him was given dominion and glory and a kingdom, that all peoples, nations, and languages should serve him; his dominion is an everlasting dominion, which shall not pass away, and his kingdom one that shall not be destroyed." (Daniel 7:13-14)

When Jesus is baptized by John the Baptist, the Father's voice from heaven confirms Jesus' identity:

"This is my beloved Son, with whom I am well pleased." (Matthew 3:17)

These hypotheses about the servant's night journey each have their supporters. Over time, however, the Umayyads used their Jerusalem Mosque to build a narrative that linked Muhammad to Abraham and embedded Islamic significance into a city already revered by Jews and Christians.

The Umayyad promotion of Jerusalem's religious significance was controversial even in their time. Some Muslim scholars thought the Qur'an was relating a dream sequence rather than a real journey. Muhammad ibn al-Hanafiya (638–700), son of Ali, dismissed the claim that Muhammad ever visited Jerusalem:

"They pretend that God [Muhammad] put his foot on the Rock in Jerusalem, though only one person ever put his foot on the rock, namely Abraham."[8]

For Israelite and Christian communities, the construction of Masjid al-Aqsa on the Temple Mount by the Umayyads was seen as a further attempt to link Muhammad to Abraham and promote Islamic claims to the Holy Land.

Persecution and the Christian Response

Over time, Islamic claims to Jerusalem solidified not only through theology but through imperial policy. This provoked rising anxiety and anger among the Christians, especially as persecution increased. Christians were restricted in their worship:

"We shall not build, in our cities or in their neighbourhood, new monasteries, churches, convents, or monks' cells, nor shall we repair, by day or by night, such of them as fall in ruins or are situated in the quarters of the Muslims." (Pact of Umar)

Under the Umayyads, suppression of other religions intensified, particularly during the reign of Caliph Abd al-Malik and his son al-Walid. Christian sites were seized and converted into mosques, as noted by historian Philip Hitti:

"From a church in Baalbek, al-Walid removed a dome of gilded brass which he set over the dome of his father's Mosque in Jerusalem. But his greatest accomplishment was the conversion in Damascus of the site of the Cathedral of St. John the Baptist, which he seized from his Christian subjects, into one of the sublimest places of worship in the world."[9]

The names of Mohammed (right) and Abu Bakr (left) now hold pride of place in the Christian Cathedral of St Sophia, Constantinople (Istanbul) / Wikimedia Commons.

Persecution escalated under later rulers, notably during the Abbasid Dynasty. Caliph Al-Hakim (996–1021) ordered the destruction of Christian churches, including the Church of the Holy Sepulchre, a church built over the burial site of Jesus. He commanded the Governor of Palestine:

"To demolish (the Sepulchre) . . . and remove its symbols, and get rid of all traces and remembrance of it."

Yaruk's son and his assistants attacked the church, looting the materials and attempting to destroy Jesus's tomb.

Naturally, when word of this desecration reached Europe, it aroused both anger and dismay. The desecration of Christian holy sites and persecution of Christians under Islamic rulers, particularly under Al-Hakim, deeply disturbed the religious conscience of medieval Europe and led to the call for the Crusades. Pope Sergius IV sent a circular letter to all churches calling for a holy fight in the Middle East and expulsion of Muslims from the Holy Land. These events would be recalled about twenty years later by Pope Urban II in his preaching for the First Crusade in 1094 AD.

The tide had turned, now it was the Christians who sought to wage a holy war. Saint Augustine of Hippo (354–430) wrote a commentary on the concept of the just war, which can be applied to the situation facing Popes Sergius IV and Urban II. In his book, *City of God*, Augustine notes:

"For it is the wrongdoing of the opposing party which compels the wise man to wage just wars…" (Book XIX, Ch. 7)

Augustine outlined that a just war must be fought for a just cause and by a legitimate authority or sovereignty. Private individuals or groups are not regarded as legitimate; only a public authority seeking peace, rather than conquest or revenge, is considered valid. The Crusades, at their inception, were wars waged by sovereigns to regain access to the Holy Land and secure peace for Christians. They were not wars of forced conversion, as faith cannot be coerced, for God gave humans free will. Faith, therefore, is a personal choice.

Understanding the Crusades, especially the First Crusade, through the lens of Augustine's just war theory sheds light on how religious and secular leaders of the day rationalized military intervention. The criteria Augustine laid out, namely a just cause, led by a legitimate authority, and pursuing peace rather than conquest provided the moral and theological grounding for action. Yet while the Crusades drew from Augustine's vision of a just war, the realities of war often fell short of its ideals, showing how the pursuit of justice can, in practice, be as fraught as the conflicts it seeks to resolve.

CHAPTER 2:
THE BIBLE

While the clash between Islam and Christianity unfolded on the battlefields and within the walls of sacred shrines, an important struggle was being played out in the realm of texts. Beneath the political conflicts over territory lay a deeper contest over authority: Which revelation was true? Which scripture could be trusted? For Christians, the Bible had always been one of the foundations of faith. For Muslims, suspicion towards the Bible as a corrupted document had long been nurtured. Thus, even as holy places were seized or defended, another campaign was being waged, this time over the soul of divine revelation itself: the Bible versus the Qur'an. For Muslims, the Bible became a book to be avoided. Yet the law of non-contradiction, the principle that two opposing claims cannot both be true, presents us with a paradox: the Gospel the Qur'an affirms is the Gospel it denies. Let us now examine these two issues: the Bible as a book to be avoided, and the Qur'anic paradox.

Why do Muslims avoid reading the Bible

Many Muslims reject the Bible and even avoid reading it because they are taught that, although God originally revealed the Scriptures, human hands later corrupted them. Concerned about this supposed corruption they avoid the Bible. Instead, they place their trust exclusively in the Qur'an because they believe it to be the perfect and final word of God, as revealed to Muhammad by an angel and compiled by his followers after his death. However, Christian scholars and even some within Islam reject this view, arguing that the Bible has remained intact.

Believers in the Bible contend that the Old and New Testaments still faithfully convey God's message. They were written in words chosen by men, for sure, but they were composed under divine inspiration and have been faithfully preserved.

This raises the question: How did the belief that the Bible was altered gain acceptance among Muslims?

The Origins of the corruption thesis

The belief that the Bible was corrupted appears to originate from a particular interpretation of a Qur'anic verse. Over time, this interpretation, became widespread in Quranic commentary (tafsir), despite its debatable accuracy. A key reference is hadith (narration) 7523 found in Sahih al-Bukhari (the authentic collection of al-Bukhari), in which it says that Abdullah ibn Abbas, a cousin of Muhammad, said:

"O group of Muslims! How can you ask the People of the Scripture about anything while your Book, which Allah has revealed to your Prophet, contains the most recent news from Allah and is pure and not distorted? Allah has informed you that the People of the Scripture changed some of Allah's words, distorted them, and wrote something with their own hands, saying, 'This is from Allah,' in order to gain a small profit. Shouldn't the knowledge that has come to you stop you from asking them? By Allah, we have never seen any of them asking you about what has been revealed to you."

The compiler of this hadith, Imam al-Bukhari (810–870), travelled across the Islamic world collecting and verifying hadiths. He finalized Sahih al-Bukhari, in Nishapur and his hometown of Bukhara, in present-day Uzbekistan.

In hadith 7523, Bukhari leaves it open to the suggestion that Ibn 'Abbas warns Muslims against seeking knowledge from the People of the Book because "they changed some of Allah's words." However, this warning seems to be based on a misinterpretation of a passage from the Qur'an which is only speaking about forgery, not textual corruption in a comprehensive sense.

"So woe to those who write the 'scripture' with their own hands, then say, 'This is from Allah,' in order to exchange it for a small price." (Qur'an 2:79)

This verse condemns forgeries, not the entire scriptural tradition. Just as the existence of counterfeit currency does not render all money worthless, so too religious scholars have historically identified false teachings while preserving authentic texts.

Another often mentioned verse says:

"There is among them a party who distort the Scripture with their tongues." (Qur'an 3:78)

However, this does not refer to textual corruption either, but to misrepresentation or misleading interpretation. The Apostle Luke records a similar warning given by the Apostle Paul:

"I know that after my departure fierce wolves will come among you…. men speaking perverse things, to draw away the disciples after them." (Acts 20:29–30)

Thus, both the Qur'an and the Bible warn against misrepresentation, not the wholesale corruption of sacred texts.

Overlooked Qur'anic Affirmations

Despite some Muslim scholars' opposition to the Bible based on hadiths, such as hadith 7523, the Qur'an itself affirms the authority of previous Scriptures:

"O People of the Scripture, you are [standing] on nothing until you uphold the Torah, the Gospel, and what has been revealed to you from your Lord." (Qur'an 5:68)

"And the word of your Lord has been fulfilled in truth and justice. None can alter His words, and He is the Hearing, the Knowing." (Qur'an 6:115)

"There is no change in the words of Allah. That is the great success." (Qur'an 10:64)

"We sent down the Torah, in which was guidance and light…" (Qur'an 5:44)

"We gave Jesus, the son of Mary, the Gospel, in which was guidance and light…" (Qur'an 5:46).

"Let the People of the Gospel judge by what Allah has revealed therein." (Qur'an 5:47)

Yet despite these clear Qur'anic affirmations of the Torah and the Gospel, later Islamic commentators increasingly advanced the doctrine of tahrif (corruption or misinterpretation) as textual corruption rather than misrepresentation, thereby discouraging Muslims from engaging with the very Scriptures the Qur'an appears to commend.

This raises two critical questions:
1. Did early Islamic authorities like Ibn 'Abbas genuinely believe that the biblical texts were altered, or has their position been reinterpreted over time?
2. What was the role of the mawali (clients/converts) in perpetrating the concept of textural corruption.

Did Ibn Abbas Believe the Bible Was Textually Corrupted?

While Sahih al-Bukhari 7523 can be interpreted to suggest that Ibn Abbas supported the theory of textual corruption, many of his closest students and their followers held a different view; namely, that the biblical Scriptures were not changed but misread.

Mujahid ibn Jabr, Ata ibn Abi Rabah, and al-Dahhak ibn Muzahim are all directly linked to Ibn Abbas either as students or theological disciples. All three emphasized the distortion of meaning, rather than the corruption of text.

It is transmitted that Mujahid ibn Jabr (642–722) said this about the relevant verse:

"'A party of them used to hear the word of Allah, then they would distort it knowingly after they had understood it' means: 'They misinterpret the words, explaining them differently from their actual meaning.'" (Sūrah Al-Baqarah, verse 75)

The idea that the Bible was just misinterpreted was also the transmitted view of Ata ibn Abi Rabah (646–733) and al-Dahhak ibn Muzahim (d. 723), both of whom taught that Jews and Christians misunderstood their Scriptures rather than tampered with them physically.

Given Ibn Abbas's students do not support the textual corruption inference in Bukhari 7523 it is reasonable to suggest that they are reflecting the view of their teacher himself.

However, over time the view that the Scriptures were corrupted, rather than misunderstood, took hold of the Islamic imagination. Later generations of Muslim converts embraced the notion of textural corruption and promoted it in their writings so that eventually it became the accepted theological position of Islam. How did this come about?

The Mawali and Early Islamic Engagement with the Bible

The 7th century Qur'an repeatedly affirmed the authority of the Torah and the Gospel as "guidance and light." For centuries the Christian Scriptures, both Old and New Testaments, had already been recognized, circulated, and faithfully preserved. The Councils of Rome, Hippo, and Carthage formally affirmed the 46 books of the Old Testament (covering the Torah and other key texts) alongside the 27 books of the New Testament. This was not a late invention; the Bible Muhammad encountered was the same text that had shaped Christian worship and theology for centuries.

Against this backdrop, early Muslim thinkers, particularly non-Arab converts or mawali, faced a dilemma. The Qur'an affirmed these Scriptures but seemed to contradict their central teachings. How could Islam affirm the Torah and Gospel yet deny what they plainly taught? This tension would lead to the claim of textual corruption (tahrif), a solution that, as we shall see, raises deeper questions about the consistency of the Qur'an's engagement with Scripture.

As Patricia Crone argues in *Slaves on Horseback*, early Islamic society, especially under the Umayyads, was structured along tribal and ethnic lines. Arab Muslims held privileged status, while non-Arab converts, the mawali, were often socially and legally subordinate, integrated as clients of Arab leaders or tribes. Many came from Jewish, Christian, or Zoroastrian backgrounds. Over time, particularly during the Abbasid period (750–861), mawali rose to prominence in scholarly and bureaucratic circles, contributing significantly to Islamic thought.

These educated converts quickly encountered a thorny problem; while the Qur'an acknowledges the Torah, Psalms, and Gospels as God's revelation, these Scriptures often contradict its own claims. The question was unavoidable: when the Qur'an says one thing and the Bible another, which should a Muslim follow and how do you explain the contradiction?

Ibn Hazm and the Doctrine of Tahrif

Muslim scholars such as Ibn Hazm proposed a simple solution. Ibn Hazm (d. 1064), was an influential Spanish theologian of Christian Persian ancestry. He declared:

"Since the Qur'an must be true, it must be that the Gospel and the Torah as they now exist are falsified. The proofs of this are the contradictions and the impossibilities they contain."

(al-Fisal fi al-Milal wa al-Ahwa' wa al-Nihal, vol. 1)

Yet Ibn Hazm's reasoning is circular; he assumes the Bible is falsified simply because it disagrees with the Qur'an. This leads to contradictions, for instance, he accepts that Isaac was the child of sacrifice, a truth found in the Torah he simultaneously claims is corrupted.

Ibn Hazm dismisses both the Scriptures themselves and the writings of early Church Fathers, relying instead on accounts from Arian Christians, whom Saint Athanasius condemned because they:

"Do not believe the Scriptures as they are, but devise for themselves strange doctrines out of them." (De Decretis, 18)

But Ibn Hazm chooses to rely on these Arian Christians who devise "strange doctrines" out of Christian scripture:

"None of the early Christian sects, such as the Arians, Paul of Samosata's followers, or the Macedonians, affirmed the Trinity or the equality of Jesus with God. Thus, the present Christian theology has no basis in their own scriptures." (al-Fisal, vol. 1)

He further claims there was only one Gospel, ignoring that the term "gospel" simply means "good news" and that multiple eyewitness accounts of Jesus' life were natural and consistent with the idea of divine testimony.

Manuscript Evidence and Biblical Stability

If the Bible had truly been altered before or after Muhammad, we would expect gaps, edits, or textual inconsistencies. But the evidence tells a different story. Manuscripts from centuries before Muhammad, including the Codex Vaticanus and Codex Sinaiticus (4th-century Greek Bibles), match today's texts line by line. The Latin Vulgate, circulating well before Islam's rise, confirms the same continuity. The Qur'an itself affirms the authority of these Scriptures:

"We sent down the Torah, in which was guidance and light…" (Qur'an 5:44)

"We gave Jesus, the son of Mary, the Gospel, in which was guidance and light…" (Qur'an 5:46)

Early commentators, such as Mujahid ibn Jabr, Ata ibn Abi Rabah, students of Ibn Abbas, and others like al-Tabari (d. 923), argued that Jews and Christians misinterpreted the Scriptures rather than corrupted them. Only later thinkers, exemplified by Ibn Hazm, claimed textual corruption, a position unsupported by Biblical manuscripts.

Revelation and the Canon

By Muhammad's time, the Christian canon, the official list of books that are recognized as divinely inspired and authoritative for faith and practice, had been recognized, translated, and widely circulated. While heretical writings, such as the Gospel of Thomas or the Gospel of Peter, circulated alongside them, the faithful had clear guidance from Church leaders who safeguarded the true Scriptures. Saint Athanasius, Patriarch of Alexandria, listed the twenty-seven New Testament books in his 39th Festal Letter (367 AD), saying about them:

"These are the fountains of salvation, that they who thirst may be satisfied with the living words they contain. In these alone is proclaimed the doctrine of godliness."

The Councils of Rome (382 AD), Hippo (393 AD), and Carthage (397, 419 AD), along with Pope Damasus's commissioning of Jerome's Latin Vulgate, confirmed these same books. Equally important, they recognized the 46 books of the Old Testament, including the Torah referenced in the Qur'an. Manuscripts from this era onward demonstrate remarkable consistency with the Bible Christians read today.

Trapped by Their Own Reasoning: Qur'anic Contradictions

This historical stability exposes a key tension; the Qur'an affirms the Scriptures while simultaneously rejecting their central claims.

To navigate this tension, early Muslim writers began to reinterpret or challenge key Biblical claims and later commentary recast central moments of the Christian story, presenting alternative accounts or questioning traditional interpretations. These reinterpretations focus on foundational Christian doctrines, including:

The identity of Abraham's child of promise – Isaac or Ishmael

The coming of the Holy Spirit at Pentecost

The nature of Jesus as divine or merely a prophet

Mary as Theotokos or a righteous woman

The significance of the Crucifixion for salvation

The sanctity of marriage as a covenant or a dissolvable contract

The framing of jihad as spiritual versus militarized struggle

These revisions were not just alternative readings; they are deliberate theological strategies, aligning the biblical narrative with Qur'anic theology.

Fundamentally, Islam's stance on the Bible runs aground on the law of non-contradiction, the principle that two opposing claims cannot both be true. The Qur'an declares the Torah and the Gospel to be "guidance and light," urging Muhammad's followers to consult them as divine revelation. Yet in the same breath, it rejects their central testimony.

If the Scriptures were uncorrupted in Muhammad's time, then the Qur'an contradicts the very revelations it commands Muslims to uphold. If they were corrupted beforehand, then the Qur'an commends as holy what it elsewhere condemns as false. Both cannot be true. If the contradiction between Qur'an and Bible reveals anything, it is that man, not God, is the author of contradiction, because there can be no contradiction in God.

The later Muslim claim of textual corruption, therefore, appears less as a historical discovery than as a theological repair, a human attempt to reconcile irreconcilable claims. It suggests that later interpreters, confronted by contradiction, tried to defend their doctrine by rewriting history. The problem, then, is not divine inconsistency, but human reasoning contradicting divine revelation.

The story of Abraham's "only son" is the first striking example of this pattern, a deliberate reshaping of revelation to fit human lineage and political and religious claims.

Isaac or Ishmael: Who was the child of sacrifice?

Many Muslims believe Ishmael, not Isaac, was the son whom God asked Abraham to sacrifice on Mount Moriah. However, the Book of Genesis clearly records God's words to Abraham:

"Take your son, your only son, whom you love, Isaac, and go to the region of Moriah. Sacrifice him there as a burnt offering on a mountain I will show you." (Genesis 22:2)

How, then, did it come about that Muslims came to believe Ishmael was the sacrificial son?

This belief likely developed after the Umayyad period (661–750 CE), as Muslim scholars aimed at strengthening Islam's claim to be the fulfillment of God's covenant with Abraham. Initially, these changes appeared as little more than speculative alternatives to the historical account recorded in Genesis, but over the centuries, what began as an hypothesis gradually solidified into established doctrine, while earlier interpretations were increasingly marginalized, or even declared heretical.

What was once an accepted "truth," that Abraham offered Isaac, was eventually overturned in favour of a "new truth", that Ishmael was the sacrifice, either on Mount Moriah or, in later Islamic tradition, at Mina near Mecca, depending on the storyteller or compiler of hadith.

Andi Azhari and Ahmed Hamdi[10] have traced the change in Muslim opinion about who was the intended sacrifice on Mount Moriah. They contend that during the first four centuries Muslim scholars such as al-Suddi, Ibn Jurayj, Muqatil ibn Sulayman, al-Tabari, and al-Samarqandi favoured the Bible account where Isaac is the sacrificial son. One of the earliest and most respected authorities on Islam, al-Tabari (839–923), reported that Ibn Abbas explicitly stated that the sacrificial son was Isaac. Al-Tabari records:

"The one whom Allah commanded to be sacrificed was Isaac. This was the view of Ibn Abbas, as well as a group from among the Companions of the Prophet."

By the 12th Century, however, commentators such as Ibn Atiyyah and al-Baghawi began to either adopt a more neutral stance or lean toward Isaac's half-brother, Ishmael, as the sacrificial offering.

By the 14th Century Scholars such as Ibn Taymiyyah and Ibn Kathir not only supported this opinion but also condemned the earlier Isaac interpretation as heretical.

This new 14th Century position stood in sharp contrast to the account preserved in Genesis, which records

Abraham building an altar to sacrifice his only son, Isaac. Isaac is described as Abraham's "only son" not in terms of biological birth order, but because he would carry forward God's covenant (promise) with Noah and Abraham. God sealed His Covenant with Noah by placing a rainbow in the sky. God sealed His Covenant with Abraham by promising Abraham a son by his elderly wife Sarah. Isaac was the firstborn son of Abraham because he was the child promised by God, a new covenant as symbolic and eternal as a rainbow.

When Abraham demonstrated his faith, an angel intervened, providing a ram in place of his son. This episode also emphasises that God desires not child sacrifice, as practiced by Abraham's pagan neighbours, but a humble and obedient heart, and the symbolic sacrifice of animals.

The Biblical account of Abraham's near-sacrifice, found in Genesis 22, is clear enough. God commands Abraham to offer "your son, your only son, Isaac, whom you love" on Mount Moriah, later associated with Jerusalem.

The Qur'an describes the son of sacrifice as a "forbearing boy" (Sura 37:101), without explicitly naming him. Islamic tradition later identifies this child as Ishmael, but this interpretation not only contradicts the explicit naming of Isaac in Genesis but also contradicts St. Paul who mentions these events in his letters to the Romans and Galatians, where he identifies Isaac as the child of promise, born "according to the Spirit," in contrast to Ishmael, who was born "according to the flesh" (Gal. 4:23). In addition, the attribute of forbearance, which the Qur'an uses ambiguously, fits more appropriately with the biblical portrait of Isaac; who, in Jewish and Christian tradition, willingly submitted to being bound on the altar, trusting in his father and in God.

According to the Torah, Isaac was the son of promise, God's chosen heir to Abraham, over Ishmael, who was born according to the flesh. The shift in Islamic tradition which isn't supported with any clarity by the Qur'an, nor by early Islamic scholars, does not represent continuity with earlier revelation, but a theological and historical departure from it.

Just as the covenant was established through Isaac, the child of promise rather than of human choice, so too the mission of the Church was inaugurated not by human will, but by divine initiative at Pentecost, when the Spirit of God was poured out, fulfilling what the earlier revelations had foreshadowed.

Pentecost and the Holy Spirit

Islamic scholars have often linked Pentecost to Muhammad, interpreting a passage from the Qur'an as a reference to him:

"Jesus [Isa] said, 'When the Comforter has come, the Spirit of Truth, [Gabriel] he will teach you all things.' And thus, the Trustworthy Spirit has brought the Qur'an down upon your heart, O Muhammad, as a detailed explanation of all things, and indeed it is mentioned in the former scriptures." (Surah Ash-Shu'ara 26:193)

However, this interpretation is problematic. The original Arabic phrase, "The Trustworthy Spirit has brought it down", does not specify Gabriel (Jibreel). Muslim scholars have inserted Gabriel's name in brackets, but this is an interpretation, not a direct translation. In addition, this claim conflicts with the Gospel's account of Pentecost and the role of the Holy Spirit.

The Role of Gabriel in Scripture

Gabriel is only mentioned twice in the New Testament and in both instances, he is only a messenger:

Firstly, when he appears to Zechariah, foretelling the birth of John the Baptist.

Then at the Annunciation, when he tells Mary, "The Holy Spirit will come upon you." (Luke 1:35)

Neither of these instances connects Gabriel to Pentecost, Gabriel is an angelic messenger, not the Holy Spirit. Yet, Islamic commentators turn Gabriel into the Holy Spirit and attempt to use John's Gospel to justify their reading of Surah 26:193. This suggests a misunderstanding of Scripture.

The True Meaning of Pentecost

John the Baptist prophesied the coming of the Holy Spirit when he declared:

"[Jesus] will baptize you with the Holy Spirit and fire." (Matthew 3:11)

Jesus confirmed this promise in the days leading up to His crucifixion. During the Feast of Tabernacles, a festival that included a significant water-drawing ritual, Jesus stood and proclaimed:

"If anyone thirsts, let him come to me and drink. He who believes in me, as the Scripture has said, 'Out of his heart shall flow rivers of living water.'" (John 7:37-38)

Jesus uses the imagery of water to remind the Israelites of the time when Moses drew water from a rock to quench their thirst, and the time when Ezekiel received a vision in which streams of living water (grace) flow out from the Temple.

Jesus also uses the imagery of the rock as a metaphor for the new Temple, the Church, and its foundation stone, the Apostle Peter: "On this rock I will build my Church." (Matt. 16:18) and from this rock "will flow rivers of living water."

The Apostle John points out this living water will flow after the resurrection of Jesus:

"Now this he said about the Spirit, which those who believed in Him were to receive; for as yet the Spirit had not been given, because Jesus was not yet glorified." (John 7:39)

Then, after His resurrection Jesus says to His Apostles:

"Go therefore and make disciples of all nations, baptizing them in the name of the Father and of the Son and of the Holy Spirit." (Matthew 28:19)

Thus, signifying the trinitarian nature of God!

The Descent of the Holy Spirit

On Pentecost, Jesus' promise is fulfilled when tongues of fire appear over the Apostles, and the Holy Spirit descends upon them. The Spirit, the eternal love between the Father and the Son, was sent from heaven to complete Jesus' teaching ministry. It gave the Apostles a faithful understanding of His message and ensured that the true Gospel would be accurately transmitted through apostolic succession. The guidance of the Spirit is Christ's guarantee that the gospel will not be corrupted, distorted, or misunderstood by the ordained ministers of the Church during her earthly pilgrimage.

This divine guidance is why Peter warns against private interpretation of Scripture:

"No prophecy of Scripture is a matter of one's own interpretation." (2 Peter 1:20)

The authority to interpret Scripture was entrusted to the Apostles and their successors, not to any self-appointed individuals. There is no universal ordained priesthood of believers; priests are anointed through apostolic succession. However, there is the common priesthood of all the baptised. All are called to offer their lives to God, to spread the faith and build the kingdom of God.

No Connection to Muhammad

There is no link between Pentecost and the Qur'anic claim that John's Gospel refers to Gabriel announcing Muhammad's claim to prophethood 600 years later. Luke was recording an event that had already occurred, the Holy Spirit's descent upon the Apostles at Pentecost, and explaining how this guidance would continue through apostolic succession.

So, a question remains to be answered: Which spirit illuminated Muhammad?

Yuhana ibn Mansur ibn Sarjun, better known as Saint John of Damascus (575 – 749), had formulated an opinion.

The nature of Jesus: divine or merely a prophet

Living under Muslim rule in the heart of Damascus, Saint John of Damascus was an administrator, theologian and defender of the Church; he saw something familiar in Islam's message. It was not a wholly new faith, he argued, but a resurrection of an ancient heresy called Arianism.

Arius, the fourth-century priest who created controversy in the early Church by teaching that Jesus was not truly divine, but rather a created being, exalted yet subordinate to God.

To the Damascene, Islam was Arianism reborn. Muhammad, he claimed, had absorbed Christian ideas filtered through heretical lenses, particularly those of an Arian monk. The result was a religion that honoured Jesus as a prophet, called Him the Word and Spirit of God, yet denied His divine sonship and His crucifixion. The Damascene wrote:

"There is also the superstition of the Ishmaelites… They are also called Saracens, which is derived from 'Sarras kenoi,' meaning 'destitute of Sarah,' in reference to what Hagar said to the angel: 'Sarah hath left me destitute'…

A false prophet named Ahmed [i.e., Muhammad, meaning the Praised One] has appeared in their midst. This man, after having chanced upon the Old and New Testaments and likewise, it seems, having conversed with an Arian monk, devised his own heresy. Ahmed says that Christ is the Word of God and His Spirit, but a creature and a servant, and that He was begotten, without seed, of Mary, the sister of Moses and Aaron. For, he says, the Word of God and the Spirit entered into Mary, and she brought forth Jesus, who was a prophet and servant of God. He further claims that the Jews sought to crucify Him in violation of the law, but that they only seized His shadow and crucified it instead. Christ Himself, he says, was neither crucified nor did He die, for God, out of His love for Him, took Him up to heaven."[11]

In the Damascene's eyes, the heresy that once threatened the Church from within had returned in another form and threatened the Church from without; it was speaking through the pages of the Qur'an.

The Qur'an's Accusation Against Christianity

On one hand, the Qur'an explicitly commands Jews and Christians to uphold their Scriptures:

"O People of the Scripture, you are standing on nothing until you uphold the Torah, the Gospel, and what has been revealed to you from the Lord." (Qur'an 5:68)

Such a statement appears to affirm that the Gospel, as it existed in the 7th century, was still authoritative and worthy of obedience. On the other hand the Qur'an directly rejects the heart of the Gospel message, that Jesus is the divine Son of God. It accuses Christians of shirk (associating partners with Allah):

"They have attributed to Allah partners—the jinn—while He has created them, and have fabricated for Him sons and daughters. Exalted is He and high above what they describe." (Qur'an 6:100)

This rejection is reinforced in a rhetorical exchange where God is depicted questioning Jesus:

"Was it you who told people, 'Consider me and my mother as gods, in addition to Allah?'"

Jesus replies: "May You be glorified! I could never say what I have no right to say... You know what is in my soul, but I do not know what is in Yours." (Qur'an 5:116)

From a Christian perspective, this is more than theological disagreement, it is an attack on the Gospel's central truth about the divine sonship of Christ and His unique role in salvation. The Qur'an tells Christians to uphold the Gospel (5:68) while simultaneously undermining the very message that defines it (5:116). If Islam teaches that God is perfect and free from contradiction, this juxtaposition poses a theological problem: how can the same God both affirm and deny the Gospel?

The Damascene wondered if this was simply an inconsistency in Muhammad's message, or did those who later compiled and arranged the Qur'an shape its message to close down debate on the most contentious issues? For the Damascene, the answer was clear, this was the voice of an old heresy reborn, one that sought to rewrite the Christian faith under the guise of affirming it.

If the Qur'an rejects the Gospel's central claim, that Jesus is the eternal Son of God, then the question naturally follows; what did Jesus Himself say about His identity? Christianity does not rest on later theological invention, but on Christ's own testimony, spoken in front of His apostles, His accusers, and even the patriarchs themselves.

Jesus Testifies to His Own Divinity

The claim that Jesus is God is not a doctrine manufactured by later church councils. It rests on the words and actions of Christ Himself, words that reach back to Abraham and Moses as His witnesses.

After healing a man on the Sabbath, Jesus is accused of blasphemy for calling God His Father. His response is striking:

"Do not think that I shall accuse you to the Father. There is one who accuses you, Moses, in whom you hope. For if you believed Moses, you would believe Me also, for he wrote of Me. But if you do not believe his writings, how will you believe My words?" (John 5:45–47)

Moses lived some 1,400 years before Jesus, yet Jesus declares that Moses wrote about Him. In the Old Testament, we read that God spoke to Moses from a burning bush and later "face to face":

"The Lord spoke to Moses face to face, as one man speaks to another." (Exodus 33:11)

Yet elsewhere God tells Moses:

"You cannot see My face, for no one may see Me and live." (Exodus 33:20)

Christians understand this apparent paradox to mean that Moses was speaking not to the Father, whom no one can see, but to Christ, the eternal Word of God before His incarnation. Saint Paul affirms this when he writes:

"For in Christ all the fullness of the Deity lives in bodily form." (Colossians 2:9)

Saint Irenaeus (c. 120–202) draws the same conclusion:

"The writings of Moses are Christ's own words. He shows this Himself when He says to the Jews… 'If you believed Moses, you would believe Me, for he wrote of Me…' He makes it abundantly clear that the writings of Moses are His [Christ's] own words."[12]

Jesus also claimed to have known Abraham personally:

"You are not yet fifty years old, and have you seen Abraham?" they asked.

His reply could not have been more direct:

"Truly, truly, I say to you, before Abraham was, I AM." (John 8:58)

By using "I AM," Jesus deliberately identified Himself with the divine name revealed to Moses:

"I AM WHO I AM." (Exodus 3:14)

In this, Jesus was not merely claiming to be a prophet; He was claiming to be God Himself.

And didn't the prophet Isaiah predict that God would become man when he declared:

"Not an elder or an angel, but the Lord Himself shall deliver them… Then the lame man shall leap like a stag, and the tongue of the dumb shall be intelligible." (Isaiah 35:5–6)

And who was it who made the lame walk and the mute speak? It was Jesus, fulfilling Isaiah's prophecy in His own ministry.

For the Damascene, Islam's rejection of Christ's divinity was nothing new. It was the revival of an ancient error, a branch grafted onto the old vine of Arianism, denying that the Word was God and claiming that the Holy Spirit was merely the angel Gabriel. Such teaching had been refuted centuries earlier at the Council of Nicaea, yet here it was again, now proclaimed by Muhammed as a new "revelation."

The Council of Nicaea

If Christ Himself testifies to His own divinity, why does Islam still deny it? Muslim scholars often argue that the doctrine of the Trinity was not part of Jesus's original teaching at all, but a later invention of the Church Fathers at the Council of Nicaea in 325. According to this claim, the 318 bishops gathered there replaced Jesus's "pure" message of monotheism with a new theology He never taught.

To support this, Muslims sometimes point to verses such as John 6:38, where Jesus says:

"For I have come down from heaven, not to do my will but to do the will of him who sent me."

They argue this proves Jesus was only a man, since He submitted to God's will. But Christians respond that because Jesus has two natures, human and divine, His human nature freely submitted to the divine will in all things. As John writes:

"The Word became flesh and dwelt among us" (John 1:14).

In the flesh, His human will perfectly aligned with the will of the Father. Thus, when He prayed in Gethsemane, "not my will, but yours be done," He was not denying His divinity but showing the obedience of a perfect human nature to the divine. Many centuries later, Thomas Aquinas reflected on this truth:

"Because He has two natures, whatever is proper to either nature can be predicated of the person of Christ." (Summa Theologiae III, q.16, a.4)

The Church Fathers of the early centuries constantly engaged with those who denied Christ's full divinity, recognising that the Arian view, which reduced Jesus to a created being or demi-god, undermined the Gospel. This theological crisis ultimately led to the convening of the Council of Nicaea in 325, and later the Council of Constantinople in 381.

At Nicaea and Constantinople, the bishops sought to safeguard the apostolic faith by formulating a creed that reaffirmed what the Church had always taught by word of mouth and by letter. They followed the Apostle Paul's exhortation to the Thessalonians:

"Stand firm, then, brothers, and keep the traditions that we taught you, whether by word of mouth or by letter." (2 Thessalonians 2:15)

The result was the Nicene Creed, a definitive statement of Christian belief, drawn from the gospels, the letters, and just as importantly, from the traditions passed on by "by word of mouth" and preserved by the Church:

"I believe in one God, the Father almighty, maker of heaven and earth, of all things visible and invisible.

I believe in one Lord Jesus Christ, the Only Begotten Son of God, born of the Father before all ages.

God from God, Light from Light, true God from true God, begotten, not made, consubstantial with the Father; through Him all things were made.

For us men and for our salvation He came down from Heaven, and by the Holy Spirit was incarnate of the Virgin Mary, and became man.

For our sake He was crucified under Pontius Pilate, suffered death, and was buried.

On the third day He rose again in accordance with the Scriptures.

He ascended into heaven and is seated at the right hand of the Father.

He will come again in glory to judge the living and the dead, and His kingdom will have no end.

I believe in the Holy Spirit, the Lord, the giver of life, who proceeds from the Father and the Son,

who with the Father and the Son is adored and glorified, who has spoken through the prophets.

I believe in one, holy, catholic, and apostolic Church, the forgiveness of sins, the resurrection of the body and life everlasting."

The Nicene Creed left no room for the Arian claim that Jesus was merely a created being. Despite these reaffirmations, Arianism maintained a strong following across the Christian world.

As the influence of Islam grew, The Damascene sought to defend the faith against the new theological challenges posed by Islam. Writing under Islamic rule in the 8th century, The Damascene In, *Exposition of the Orthodox Faith*, affirmed both the unity of God and the three divine Persons:

"We do not speak of three Gods but of one God... the Father, the Son, and the Holy Spirit, one in essence, distinguished in persons." (Exposition, I.8)

The Damascene was only affirming what Scripture proclaims:

"Go therefore and make disciples of all nations, baptizing them in the name of the Father, and of the Son, and of the Holy Spirit." (Matthew 28:19)

"The grace of the Lord Jesus Christ, and the love of God, and the fellowship of the Holy Spirit be with you all." (2 Corinthians 13:14)

Here Paul blesses the Church in the name of three distinct persons, each active and divine. The Trinity is not a council's creation as Muslims are taught, but the Church's faithful reading of Scripture.

The Scriptures themselves also pointed to the Trinitarian nature of God because it was first revealed in Genesis (Torah) when God said to another, "Let *us* make mankind in *our* image and likeness." (Genesis 1:26)

The Gospel of John identifies Christ as the person God spoke to in Genesis, calling Him the Word:

"In the beginning was the Word, and the Word was with God, and the Word was God. All things were made through him." (John 1:1-3)

And later, John explicitly affirms Christ's incarnation:

"And the Word became flesh and dwelt among us."
(John 1:14)

The Church Fathers stood firm in the Apostolic tradition, rejecting those who distorted Christian teaching, especially those who attributed false words to Christ and His mother:

"Was it you who told people, 'Consider me and my mother as gods, in addition to Allah?'" (Qur'an 5:116)

Yet, no Christian has ever claimed Mary is a deity. Mary is the daughter of Anne and Joachim. This passage raises a critical question: Is this verse in the Qur'an meant to refute Mary's title of Theotokos, the "God-bearer"? This title was popular among the early Christians and was affirmed by the Church, especially in Byzantium.

Mary: The God-bearer (Theotokos) or righteous woman?

In the Christian faith, no figure is more revered among women than Mary, the mother of Jesus. Yet, this reverence has often been misunderstood, particularly in Islamic society when they mistake honour for idolatry. The Qur'an appears to be responding to something Christians never actually claimed, that Mary is part of the Trinity. But the Church has never deified Mary. She is not God, but she is, without hesitation, the Theotokos.

This title was foreshadowed by the prophet Isaiah, fulfilled when the Angel Gabriel visited Mary and reaffirmed at the Council of Ephesus in 431.

The prophet Isaiah had already pointed to Mary's pivotal role centuries earlier.

"The Lord himself therefore, will give you a sign. It is this; the maiden is with child and will soon give birth to a son whom she will call Emmanuel, a name which means, "God is with us." (Isaiah 7:14)

This prophecy was fulfilled when the angel Gabriel appeared to Mary:

"Hail, full of grace, the Lord is with thee... Behold, thou shalt conceive in thy womb and bring forth a son; and thou shalt call his name Jesus. He shall be great and shall be called the Son of the Most High." (Luke 1:28-32)

Perplexed, Mary asked how this could be, given that she was a virgin. Gabriel reassured her:

"The Holy Spirit will come upon you, and the power of the Most High will overshadow you; therefore, the child to be born will be called holy, the Son of God." (Luke 1:35)

This narrative, obviously based on Mary's own testimony, was later altered in the Qur'an:

"My Lord! How can I have a child when no man has touched me?" [The angel] replied: "Such is the will of Allah. He creates what He wills. When He decrees a thing, He only says: 'Be!' - and it is." (Qur'an 3:47)

In the Qur'anic version, the miraculous conception is retained, but the underlying theology shifts. Jesus is not the eternal Son who "comes down from heaven" (John 6:38); rather, he is created in time by divine fiat, "Be, and it is." This reflects something much closer to the Arian heresy, which claimed that the Son of God was not eternal, but made.

And yet Jesus Himself refutes this idea:

"Before Abraham was, I am." (John 8:58)

A created being does not speak this way. Only the eternal Word, who was with God and was God (John 1:1), can make such a claim.

The Council of Ephesus and the Theotokos

Having defended Christ's full divinity at Nicaea, the Church soon faced a new challenge; one that threatened to divide His humanity from His divinity. At the centre of this controversy stood Mary's title of Theotokos, the "God-bearer."

This title, foreshadowed by Isaiah and fulfilled in Gabriel's message to Mary, had long been used by Christians in prayer and liturgy. But in 431 it became the focal point of a major theological dispute. The Council of Ephesus was convened to settle the growing controversy ignited by Nestorius, the Patriarch of Constantinople. Nestorius insisted that Mary should not be called Theotokos but rather Christotokos, "Mother of Christ," arguing that Mary gave birth only to Christ's human nature, not His divine.

However, Cyril, the Patriarch of Alexandria, countered that Church tradition affirmed Mary as Theotokos because Christ's two natures, human and divine, were united in one person. Since motherhood applies to persons, not natures, it was entirely appropriate to call Mary the Mother of God. For Cyril and the catholic and apostolic tradition he upheld, to deny Mary the title Theotokos was to deny the unity of Christ's person. Cyril wrote to Nestorius, urging him to reconsider:

"To say that the Word became flesh is the same as saying that He became a sharer in flesh and blood (Hebrews 2:14). He took our body for His own and, as man, was born of a woman—without losing His divinity or His birth from the Father, but remaining what He was, even when He assumed flesh.

This is the faith of the Church, affirmed by the holy Fathers. That is why they do not hesitate to call the holy Virgin Theotokos—not because the divine nature of the Word took its origin from her, but because He took His holy body, gifted with a rational soul, from her. Since the Word is hypostatically united to this body, we can truly say that He was born according to the flesh.

I write these things, compelled by the love of Christ, exhorting you as a brother to believe and teach these truths with us, so that peace may be preserved among the Churches, and the bond of unity among God's priests may remain unbroken." (Letter 2 to Nestorius)

Despite Cyril's appeal, Nestorius refused to yield and continued to insist that Mary should be called Christotokos.

The Role of the Bishop of Rome

Both Cyril and Nestorius turned to the Bishop of Rome for support. The Bishop of Rome, successor of Saint Peter and guardian of apostolic tradition was widely acknowledged as primus inter pares (first among equals) among the patriarchs. For Jesus had said to Peter:

"You are Peter, and upon this rock I will build my Church... Whatever you bind on earth will be bound in heaven." (Matthew 16:19)

At the time, Pope Celestine I occupied the See of Peter. He convened a synod (assembly) of bishops in Rome, which upheld the Church's tradition and confirmed that Mary should rightly be called Theotokos. He wrote to Nestorius, urging him to submit to the apostolic faith.

But Nestorius refused. Instead of accepting the judgment of the Church, he turned to the imperial court in Constantinople and appealed to Emperor Theodosius II dragging a question of theological doctrine into the arena of imperial politics.

The Council of Ephesus

In response, Emperor Theodosius II called for a Council to be held in Ephesus to settle the matter. Pope Celestine did not attend but sent representatives, delegating Cyril as his official spokesman:

"We have delegated our holy brother Cyril in our place."[13]

Despite Nestorius's political manoeuvring and the late arrival of a group of Arian bishops, the Council overwhelmingly sided with Cyril. The bishops formally condemned Nestorius's teaching and confirmed the Church's tradition: Mary is Theotokos, the God-Bearer.

Now, centuries after the Council of Ephesus, the Damascene found himself once again defending this doctrine, this time against a new wave of Arab Arians who sought to deny the prophetic foreshadowing of Isaiah, the message of Gabriel, and Church tradition.

Not only did the Qur'an reject Mary's title as Theotokos, but it also went further and denied Christ's crucifixion altogether, claiming instead that it was only His shadow (His appearance), not Jesus Himself, who was crucified.

The Crucifixion

Islam rejects the historical reality of Jesus's crucifixion, asserting in the Qur'an:

"And because of their saying: We slew the Messiah, Jesus son of Mary, Allah's messenger." They slew him not, nor crucified him, but it appeared so to them; and those who disagree concerning it are in doubt thereof; they have no knowledge thereof except pursuit of a conjecture; they slew him not for certain." (Q 4:157)

A Qur'anic commentary explains:

"Allah saved Noah from the flood; Abraham from the fire, Muhammed from the traps of the idolators, and Jesus from the wickedness of the Jews, who wished to crucify him. It was Judas Iscariot, who sought to betray Jesus, who was arrested instead, and crucified instead of the Prophet Jesus, upon whom be peace."

Islam's rejection of Jesus's crucifixion contradicts the Scriptures and the historical records. Tacitus confirms the Romans killed Jesus because they regarded Him as the leader of a dangerous sect. Tacitus mentions Jesus's death while describing how Emperor Nero blamed Christians for the outbreak of a fire in Rome in the year 64:

"Nero fastened the guilt and inflicted the most exquisite tortures on a class hated for their abominations, called Christians by the populace. Christus, from whom the name had its origin, suffered the extreme penalty during the reign of Tiberius at the hands of one of our procurators, Pontius Pilatus, and a most mischievous superstition, thus checked for the moment, again broke out not only in Judea, the first source of the evil, but even in Rome."[14]

The "superstition" certainly broke out again in Judea because after His resurrection Jesus regularly appeared to His friends, including the Apostles on Easter Sunday, when they were discussing news about Him from the village of Emmaus. He broke bread at Emmaus with two of His followers saying to them, "Everything written about Me in the law of Moses and the prophets and the psalms must be fulfilled." Psalm 22 was certainly fulfilled: "They have pierced my hands and my feet…. They divided my garments among them."

"They were still talking about all this when Jesus himself stood among them and said, "Peace be with you!" In a state of alarm and fright, they thought they were seeing a ghost. But he said, "Why are you so agitated, and why are these doubts rising in your hearts? Look at my hands and my feet, it is I indeed. Touch me and see for yourselves; a ghost has no flesh and no bones as you can see, I have." (Luke 24:36-49)

And then came Pentecost. The Holy Spirit descended upon the Apostles, fulfilling Christ's promise and empowering them to proclaim this Good News; that the crucified and risen Christ is Lord of all, and that through Him alone, salvation has come to the world.

Why Would Islam Deny the Cross?

From a Christian point of view, the crucifixion of Jesus is not just a historical event, it is the hinge of salvation history, the culmination of the prophets' witness, and the act by which the world is redeemed. So, when Islam categorically denies this event, the Christian is left asking: Why?

Why would a religion that claims continuity with the biblical prophets, even honouring Jesus as a great messenger, reject the very act that defines His mission? Various reasons can be put forward.

By the time the Qur'an was being compiled and recited in 7th-century Arabia, Islam was positioning itself as the true heir to the Abrahamic tradition. It affirmed Moses and Jesus, but redefined them under a new revelation that centred on Muhammad as God's final and greatest prophet. To acknowledge the cross would be to affirm the central claim of the Gospel, that Jesus is not just a prophet, but the crucified and risen Son of God. Islam could not do that without collapsing its own foundation.

The Qur'anic denial of the crucifixion also supports a Muslim observation, namely that God always saves His prophets. Noah was saved from the flood, Abraham from the fire, and Muhammad from assassination attempts. In the same way Jesus too must be "saved," not sacrificed (John the Baptist wasn't so lucky!). Thus, the cross becomes a scandal that must be erased, not a sign to be lifted up (John 3:14).

Finally, Islamic scholars like Ibn Hazm in the 11th century promoted the claim that the Gospel accounts were corrupted, probably after Muhammed's time; a view that justified the Qur'an's divergence from biblical testimony.

Yet this doctrine of tahrif (textual corruption) only appears in Islamic thought after it became clear that the Qur'an could not be harmonized with the Gospels. However, as already noted, if, as claimed, the scriptures were altered after Muhammed's time, why is the Qur'an rejecting Scripture from the Bible available in Muhammed's time, which supposedly wasn't corrupted.

The Qur'an's assertion that Jesus was not crucified, but that "it appeared so," (Qur'an 4:157) has puzzled and troubled Christian thinkers for centuries. Early Christian apologists, like the Damascene, recognized in this denial an echo of old heresies, teachings the Church had long rejected as false.

So where did this claim come from? And what motivated it?

There are at least two major explanations, the first concerns Gnostic influences that may have filtered into early Islamic thought. The second concerns the deeper doctrinal divide between Islam and Christianity, especially over the nature of salvation and the meaning of grace.

Let us begin with the first.

One explanation for Islam's denial of the crucifixion points to a second century Egyptian gnostic monastic text which bears similarities to Qur'an 4:157. Some authorities believe the Gnostic account influenced Islams rejection of the crucifixion. The text is called the Second Treatise of the Great Seth and in part it says:

"I [Jesus] did not succumb to them as they had planned … And I did not die in reality but in appearance, lest I be put to shame by them … For my death which they think happened, (happened) to them in their error and blindness, since they nailed their man unto their death… It was another, their

father, who drank the gall and the vinegar; it was not I…
It was another, Simon, who bore the cross on his shoulders.
It was another upon whom they placed the crown of thorns."

Gnosticism, which emphasizes secret knowledge (gnosis) and often denied the physical reality of Christ, was rejected as heretical by the early Church. The Qur'anic rejection of the crucifixion appears to echo this Gnostic belief, which viewed Jesus as a purely spiritual being, incapable of suffering a physical death.

The old Gnostic religion believed gnosis led to spiritual enlightenment and salvation, thus the popularity of modern gurus who continue the gnostic tradition by promising self-fulfilment programs. Gnosticism saw the material world as evil and the early Church responded by saying when God filled the earth with all kinds of living creatures, He "saw that it was good." Furthermore, true gnosis (knowledge) is available through the Scriptures, the teachings of the Church Fathers and their successors, under the guidance of the Holy Spirit.

A second explanation centres on a theological difference: Christianity teaches that Jesus offered Himself as a sacrificial lamb for the redemption of mankind, fulfilling Isaiah's prophecy:

"We like sheep have gone astray, every one has turned aside into his own way: and the Lord has laid on him the iniquity of us all." (Isaiah 53:6)

Islam, however, rejects this redemptive sacrifice. A Qur'anic commentary states:

"Any other view of redemption [other than Jihad] is rejected by Islam, especially the corrupted form of Christianity which thinks that some other person suffered for our sins, and we are redeemed by his blood." (Commentary on Q 9:111)

This perspective on redemption stands in contrast to Christian teachings, which emphasize salvation through Christ's sacrifice. To better understand these differences the nature of salvation in both traditions needs to be understood.

The Nature of Salvation: Christianity vs. Islam

Islamic theology asserts that salvation is achieved through personal effort, particularly jihad (spiritual or military struggle). This view resembles the teachings of the English monk Pelagius (355-425), who argued that people could attain salvation through their own efforts. The Council of Carthage (418) condemned Pelagianism saying:

"Whoever says that the grace of justification is given as a reward for human merit, let him be anathema." (Canon 8)

The council sent its decisions to Pope Zosimus in Rome. Zosimus, after reviewing the African bishops' evidence issued the Epistula Tractoria, a formal papal letter condemning Pelagius and endorsing the council's teaching. All Western bishops were required to sign it.

The debate over the role of faith and personal effort (works) in Christian theology did not end in the early Church. Many centuries later, Martin Luther's insistence that we are justified by faith alone (sola fide), the exact opposite to Palagius, prompted a formal response from the Church at the Council of Trent (1545-1563). In its Decree on

Justification, the council affirmed that while faith is the beginning of salvation, it must be united with cooperation in grace:

"Faith alone does not justify us because we must cooperate with grace by preparing and disposing our will toward God's action. Faith alone does not prevent our wills from resisting God's grace. We can choose to sin; if the sin is serious, we separate ourselves from God." (paraphrase of Trent, Session VI)

The Church teaches that while good works are essential, they are a response to grace, not a means of earning salvation:

"He saved us, not because of the righteous things we had done, but because of His mercy. He saved us through the washing of rebirth (baptism) and renewal by the Holy Spirit, which He poured out on us generously through Jesus Christ our Savior." (Titus 3:5-6)

"It is God, for His own loving purpose, who puts both the will and the action into you." (Philippians 2:13)

Islam, however, took a different path, one that echoed the ancient heresy of Pelagius, offering salvation through a person's own efforts. Pelagius put all the weight on human effort, Luther put it all on faith apart from works, and the Church rejected both, holding instead to the apostolic balance: we are saved by grace alone, which should put both "the will and action into you," through faith working in love. The Church rejected Pelagianism because it knew the truth of the human condition; without God's grace, we stumble again and again, no matter how sincere our intentions. We cannot climb to heaven by our own strength; we must be lifted up. And that lifting is grace, God's own friendship, a free and undeserved gift. It is more than mere favour; it is a share in the divine nature itself.

And here lies the heart of the Christian life; grace is not just a doctrine to affirm, but a living stream that flows from Christ Himself. The question, then, is how this grace reaches us now that He has ascended to the Father.

Grace and the Sacraments

When Jesus walked this earth, He lifted people up by pouring out grace through His physical presence. He stretched out His hand and cleansed a leper. A woman touched the fringe of His cloak and "power went out from Him" to heal her. A sinful woman washed His feet with her tears, and He said, "Thy sins are forgiven thee." The Pharisees scoffed, how could He forgive a sinner? but Jesus replied that her many sins were forgiven "for she loved much." As Aquinas put it, "Whoever loves God possesses God in himself."

But now Jesus is in Heaven. So how do we touch His cloak, or hear the words, "Thy sins are forgiven"? The answer is twofold. First, we approach Him in faith, for as Blessed Columba Marmion reminds us, "A divine virtue goes out from Him and penetrates our souls to enlighten and help them." Second, He lifts us up through the seven sacraments He instituted, outward signs of inward grace, handed down to us and safeguarded by the Church Fathers. Through these, the risen Christ still reaches out His hand to heal, forgive, and raise us to share His divine life.

For instance, Jesus teaches by the water of Baptism, "we are cleansed of our sins and born to a life of grace." After His resurrection Jesus instituted the Sacrament of Reconciliation (confession) when He appeared to His Disciples and "… Breathed on them, and said to them, "Receive the Holy Spirit. If you forgive the sins of any, they are forgiven; if you retain the sins of any, they are retained." (John 20:22-23)

When announcing the Sacrament of the Eucharist Jesus says, "He who eats my flesh and drinks my blood lives in me and I live in him…. This is the bread come down from Heaven…." (John 6: 56-58). John records, "He taught this doctrine at Capernaum." Doctrine is a strong word for settled teaching and many of Jesus's followers left him because they could not accept this doctrine. They knew Jesus wasn't using figurative language; there was no allegory, no metaphor, just doctrine. They could not believe the flesh and blood sacrifice of the cross could be offered as a pascal sacrifice under the species of bread and wine. If Jesus was speaking symbolically, he would not have had a problem. But, "After this, many of His disciples left Him, and stopped going with Him." (John 6:66)

Saint Irenaeus who was taught by Saint Polycarp, who was taught by the Apostle John (a powerful chain of transmission) offers his own explanation about the Doctrine taught at Capernaum:

"The oblation of the Eucharist is not a mere symbol but a true sacrifice, as the Church has received from the apostles, and offers it to God throughout the world." (Against Heresies 4.17.5)

Saint Ambrose (339-397) offers this explanation about the "bread come down from heaven."

"Be convinced that this is not what nature has formed, but what the blessing has consecrated. The power of the blessing prevails over that of nature, because by the blessing nature itself is changed.... Could not Christ's words, which can make from nothing what did not exist, change existing things into what they were not before? It is no less a feat to give things their original nature than to change their nature."[15]

The Council of Trent explains the Eucharist as a sacrifice because it re-presents (makes present) the sacrifice of the cross:

"[Christ], our Lord and God, was once and for all to offer himself to God the father by his death on the Altar of the cross, to accomplish there an everlasting redemption. But because his priesthood was not to end with his death, at the Last Supper "on the night when he was betrayed," [he wanted] to leave his beloved spouse the Church a visible sacrifice (as the nature of man demands) by which the bloody sacrifice which he was to accomplish once for all on the cross would be re-presented, its memory perpetuated until the end of the world, and its salutary power be applied to the forgiveness of sins we daily commit."[16]

The doctrine of Capernaum as recorded in John 6, is exercised by ministers appointed by the Apostles and their successors and as Saint Irenaeus wrote:

"We must obey the presbyters in the Church. They are the successors of the Apostles, and by the Father's good pleasure, they have received, together with the succession in the episcopate, the sure charism of the truth."[17]

Saint Irenaeus cautioned against ministers not appointed by Apostolic succession:

[Those] "who have broken away from the original succession to set up in various places conventicles (meetings) of their own, are to be regarded with suspicion."[18]

Islam, though emerging centuries later, fits this description, establishing its own places of worship (mosques), separate from the apostolic tradition, and venerating distinct relics and sacred sites such as the Black Stone and the Zamzam well.

The Roots of the Islamic Tradition

To grasp how Islam came to reframe Abraham's story and create holy ground far from Hebron, we must explore the roots of Muslim tradition and the reinterpretations that shaped it.

Islam's earliest worship gatherings took place in mosques, and its first significant holy sites were the Zamzam well and the Ka'bah in Mecca. Islamic tradition strongly associates these places with Abraham. According to Qur'an 14:37, Abraham left Hagar and Ishmael in a barren valley, interpreted by later Muslim tradition as Mecca, which is some 1,400 kilometres south of Hebron, to avoid conflict with Sarah, who had demanded Hagar's dismissal after she exulted in the birth of Ishmael at Sarah's expense. Then, later on, Ishmael took it upon himself to mock Isaac. As the Apostle Paul would later reflect:

"But as at that time he who was born according to the flesh persecuted him who was born according to the Spirit, so it is now also." (Galatians 4:29)

Islamic tradition holds that Abraham made regular journeys to Mecca and eventually helped Ishmael build the Ka'bah, a cube-shaped sanctuary that, according to legend, housed a black stone said to have been given to Adam when he was expelled from Eden. Nearby, a spring miraculously appeared in the desert, where Ishmael's heel touched the ground. This spring became known as the Zamzam well.

While Surah Ibrahim 14:37 does speak of Abraham settling some of his descendants near "Your Sacred House" in a barren valley, it does not name Mecca, nor does it identify Ishmael. Given Abraham's enduring association with Hebron and Mount Moriah, Jerusalem or a nearby location is far more plausible as the original "Sacred House." The idea of replacing Jerusalem with Mecca only gained traction in later Islamic interpretive traditions. As this interpretation of Surah 14:37 became dominant, the Ka'bah and Zamzam well grew in significance.

The Biblical Account

By contrast, the biblical narrative offers no support for a 1,400-kilometre southern journey to Mecca. When Sarah sends Hagar away, Genesis records that Hagar fled toward Shur, roughly 150-200 kilometres from Hebron, on the path back to her Egyptian homeland. She was not far along this road when an angel appeared to her:

"Return to thy mistress and submit thyself under her hands." (Genesis 16:9)

Later, when Abraham dies, both Ishmael and Isaac bury him beside Sarah in the cave of Machpelah in the field of Ephron, which is just 40 kilometres south of Jerusalem in Judea (Genesis 25).

Today, that region is often referred to as the "West Bank," a term that not so subtly detaches the territory from its ancestral name, Judea, a land promised to the descendants of Isaac through whom the covenant would continue. When Islam expanded into the land between the river and the sea, it laid claim not only to Judea but to the burial ground of Abraham and asserted its lineage through Ishmael, despite Psalm 80 saying that only one vine was planted between the river and the sea:

"You [God] brought a vine out of Egypt;

To plant it you drove out the nations.

Before it you cleared the ground;

It took root and spread through the land.

… It stretched out its branches to the sea,

To the great river it stretched out its shoots."

Islam turned away from the vine brought out of Egypt and planted in Judea, forsaking a promise which was to be fulfilled in the town of Bethlehem in Judea:

"A shoot shall come out from the stump of Jesse,

And a branch shall grow out of his roots." (Isaiah 11:1)

And as the prophet Micah, who lived in the same era as Isaiah, also foretold:

"But you, Bethlehem Ephrathah, though you are small among the clans of Judah, out of you shall come for me one who is to be ruler in Israel, whose origins are from of old, *from the days of eternity*"

These prophets foretold of a vine planted in the province of Judea, destined to blossom in Bethlehem and be fulfilled in the person of Jesus Christ. This stands in stark contrast to the later Islamic shift, which transplants the Abraham's story southward, from the land of Judea to the deserts of Arabia, recasting the heir and relocating the hoped for Messiah. While Christianity sees the Abrahamic covenant resting in the Messiah born in Bethlehem; whose origins are "from the days of eternity," Islam relocates the Abraham's legacy some 1,400 kilometres southward to Mecca and repositions Ishmael as the heir.

This theological shift had profound implications beyond geography and lineage; it ended up influencing morality and social relations, especially the understanding of marriage.

If the Christian and Islamic views of salvation stand worlds apart, one grounded in grace and the other in striving, then it should come as no surprise that their understandings of human relationships diverge just as dramatically. What one believes about God inevitably shapes what one believes about love, covenant, and community.

Marriage, in this sense, becomes more than a private institution or cultural tradition. It becomes a mirror of one's theology; a reflection of how God relates to His people.

Marriage: Sacramental covenant or dissolvable contract?

For Christians, marriage is a sacramental covenant, instituted by God to reflect His own faithful love. For Muslims, marriage is often portrayed in legalistic terms, a contract that can be modified, expanded, or dissolved, even by divine concession.

Where Christianity teaches that love is the highest fulfillment of the law and grace its animating power Islam proposes a different path. Here, obedience is rooted not in adoption as sons and daughters of God, but in submission to a master, and devotion is demonstrated not through covenant, but through striving. That striving takes its clearest form in Jihad, a concept that has shaped both personal piety and public policy in the Islamic tradition from its earliest days.

What we find in comparing these two traditions is not just a difference in customs, but a fundamental disagreement about the meaning of love, the dignity of women, and the purpose of human union.

Having abandoned the true vine, Islam also abandoned the moral order it upheld, replacing the sacred covenant of marriage with man-made permissions and privileges that stood in direct contradiction to God's original plan.

In the Qur'an, Muhammad is granted special permission to marry multiple wives, while his followers can have up to four wives. In contrast, Jesus upholds monogamy and condemns divorce. He affirms the Genesis teaching on marriage, saying:

"A man will leave his father and mother and be joined to his wife, and the two will become one flesh. What God has joined, let no man separate." (Matthew 19:5-6)

Jesus speaks of a wife, not multiple wives. Yet, Muhammad had nine or more wives, including female prisoners of war. According to the Qur'an, this was a special dispensation granted to him by divine command:

"O Prophet! We have made lawful to thee thy wives to whom thou hast paid their dowers, and those whom thy right hand possesses out of the prisoners of war whom Allah has assigned to thee; and daughters of thy paternal uncles and aunts, and daughters of thy maternal uncles and aunts, who migrated (from Makka) with thee; and any believing woman who dedicates her soul to the Prophet if the Prophet wishes to wed her; this only for thee, and not for the Believers at large. ..." (Qur'an 33:50)

This allowance stands in stark contrast to the biblical account, where marriage is consistently depicted as a sacred union between one man and one woman. The Book of Genesis records:

"Therefore, a man leaves his father and his mother and clings to his wife, and they become one flesh." (Genesis 2:24)

When questioned about Moses permitting divorce, Jesus explains that it was allowed because of the hardness of people's hearts, but it was never God's original intent:

"Whoever divorces his wife, except for unchastity, and marries another commits adultery." (Matthew 19:9)

And in earlier times wasn't God's attitude made clear by the Prophet Malachi:

"So, take heed to yourselves, and let none be faithless to the wife of his youth. For I hate divorce,' says the Lord, the God of Israel." (Malachi 2:15-16)

Jesus allows for the legal separation of spouses in cases of unchastity (from the Greek porneia), which may refer to adultery or marriages deemed unlawful under Leviticus 18 when a marriage is between partners who are too closely related by blood. However, He clearly forbids remarriage. Even the Apostles are taken aback by the strictness of His teaching:

"If such is the case… it is better not to marry."

But Jesus responds by saying. "He who is able to receive this, let him receive it." (Matthew 19)

This divine framework for marriage, as revealed through Malachi and reinforced by Jesus, sets the stage for understanding not only the earthly commitment between spouses but also its implications for eternity.

Marriage in Heaven

Islam teaches that women who never marry in this life may choose a husband in paradise. However, Jesus presents a very different vision of the afterlife:

"The sons of this age marry and are given in marriage, but those who are accounted worthy to attain to that age and to the resurrection from the dead neither marry nor are given in marriage, for they cannot die anymore. They are equal to angels and are sons of God." (Luke 20:34-36)

Additionally, Islam describes paradise as a place of physical pleasures, including feasts, luxurious surroundings, and, for some, the companionship of 72 virgins. Yet, if there is no marriage in heaven, then logically, there are no concubines either.

In contrast to Islam, Christians understand heaven as the union of a person's soul with God, together with the communion of saints. God the Father explained the soul to Saint Catherine of Sienna saying:

"Heaven I call her (The Soul) because so I made her, living in her first by Grace, and hiding myself within her, and making of her a mansion through affection of love."[19]

In contrast to earthly marriage those in Heaven, although united with loved ones and friends, are no longer bound in the same way by human relationships because being made equal to angels they are fully united with God. This understanding sets the foundation for the true nature of marriage as a sacred covenant.

The Divine Order of Marriage

While marriage on earth serves as a bond of love and fidelity, Jesus reveals a deeper reality where in the resurrection earthly relationships give way to a divine unity with God. This insight transforms marriage from a mere human institution into a sacred covenant, designed by God to reflect His love and purpose. The Qur'an's views on marriage, polygamy, and captives contradict this concept of sacred covenant.

Even if one were to argue that the Qur'an's teachings on marriage were shaped by historical circumstances, such a position would be theologically flawed. God is neither confined by time nor subject to societal norms, and His will is not open to negotiation; the clay does not instruct the potter. Through Genesis, Malachi, and ultimately Jesus, God has already revealed the true nature of marriage as a monogamous, lifelong covenant.

Fundamentally, marriage should be about love, and as Saint Thomas Aquinas points out, love in God is an act, not a passion; God's love evokes and creates the goodness in things. Love means to will the good of the other, as other. God loved men and women so much He made them in His own likeness and image, and as Aquinas says, "Everything has a built-in affinity for what accords with its nature."

Because men and women bear the image of God, they are drawn to love and to act on that love. In its highest form, marriage is an act of selfless love, a partnership that desires to will the good of another by bringing forth a new eternal life when two become one flesh, willingly entering into a creative partnership with the Creator. Scripture itself gives us this image when Isaiah declares, "You shall be called, 'My Delight is in her,' and your land Married; for the Lord delights in you, and your land shall be married" (Isaiah 62:4). God's covenant with His people is pictured as a marriage, not a contract of power, but a union of delight, fidelity, and fruitfulness.

The New Testament carries this imagery further. Saint Paul, in Ephesians 5, speaks of the mystery of marriage as a reflection of Christ and the Church:

"Husbands, love your wives, as Christ loved the church and gave himself up for her…"

The bond of man and woman becomes a sacrament of the greater reality, the bridegroom who lays down His life for His bride. And the vision of Revelation reaches its climax with the New Jerusalem, "prepared as a bride adorned for her husband" (Revelation 21:2). The story of salvation, then, is framed from beginning to end as God's faithful, self-giving marriage covenant with His people.

Where Christianity teaches that love is the highest fulfillment of the law, and grace its animating power, Islam proposes a different path. Here, obedience is rooted not in adoption as sons and daughters of God, but in submission to a master, and devotion is demonstrated not through covenant, but through striving. That striving takes its clearest form in Jihad, a concept that has shaped both personal piety and public policy in the Islamic tradition from its earliest days. In Islam, the concept of jihad, derived from the Arabic root jahada meaning "to strive," lies at the heart of devotion.

Jihad: Spiritual struggle or holy war?

Jihad, in its broader religious sense, reflects the Pelagian mindset because the believer strives to obey divine commands, to perform acts of worship, to avoid sin, and, in some interpretations, to defend or expand the faith, with the hope that such efforts will tip the scales toward eternal reward.

From the earliest centuries of Islam, jurists codified jihad as a religious duty, grounding their rulings in Qur'anic commands such as, "Fight those who do not believe… until they pay the jizya" (Qur'an 9:29) and "Fight them until there is no more fitna and the religion is wholly for Allah" (Qur'an 8:39).

Malik ibn Anas (d. 795), in his al-Muwatta', includes rulings not only on military expeditions and the division of spoils, but also on non-combat matters such as the rewards for memorising Qur'anic verses or engaging in extended fasting, treating these as forms of jihad of the soul.

In all these forms, whether military or devotional, the emphasis falls on human effort as the decisive factor. Here, both the "greater" jihad (personal discipline) and the "lesser" jihad (armed struggle) fall towards the Pelagian premise; that man, by his own will and effort, can attain divine favour without the transforming gift of sanctifying grace.

The Military Struggle

If we Focus on the military aspect, often called the 'lesser jihad', we find this concept enshrined not only in Islamic scripture but also echoed in related religious traditions, which some Muslim apologists highlight to justify armed struggle.

Muslim apologists have sometimes justified military expansion by appealing to a triad of sacred texts; not only from the Qur'an, but also from the Torah and the Gospel; claiming that Jihad has precedent in all three.

Qur'an 9:111 demands Muslims fight and it says Christians and Israelites are bound to do the same:

"Indeed, Allah has purchased from the believers their lives and their properties [in exchange] for that they will have Paradise. They fight in the cause of Allah, so they kill and are killed. [It is] a true promise [binding] upon Him in the Torah and the Gospel and the Qur'an. And who is truer to his covenant than Allah? So rejoice in the bargain you have made with Him."

Muslims point to these scriptural precedents, suggesting that the call to military jihad finds echoes not just in the Qur'an but also in the Torah and the Gospel, inviting a closer look at these texts and their context.

Comparison with Israelite and Christian Scriptures

Muslims infer that Israelites are called to Jihad because in the Torah (Genesis to Deut.) God commands Israel:

"You shall consume all the nations [territory] which the Lord, your God, will deliver up to you. You are not to look on them with pity, lest you be snared into serving their Gods." (Deut. 7:16)

However, Israel's conquests have a spiritual dimension, a return to right order and harmony in God's creation. God uses Israel to remove the local Canaanite false gods because they encourage injustice by leading humanity away from God, rather than towards God. These false Gods even encouraged child sacrifice:

"Do not give any of your children to be sacrificed to Moloch, for you must not profane the name of your God." (Leviticus 18:21)

However, God puts a limit on the lands Israel may conquer, after which Israel will be a "light for revelation to the gentiles" and streams of living water will flow out from the Temple as the Holy Spirit speaks through the prophets. As the Apostle Paul tells the Hebrews:

"At various times in the past and in various different ways, God spoke to our ancestors through the prophets; but in our own time, the last days, He has spoken to us through his son." (Hebrews 1:1-2)

Muslims sometimes cite Jesus's words, "I came not to bring peace but a sword," (Matthew 10:34) as evidence of Christian justification for violence. But this interpretation collapses when the broader context is considered. The "sword" here is not steel but division, the painful rupture that occurs when the Gospel challenges family loyalties, cultural norms, and worldly comforts. Jesus Himself clarifies this when, facing death, He rebukes Peter for taking up the sword:

"Put your sword back into its place, for all who take the sword will perish by the sword" (Matthew 26:52).

Luke also records Jesus rebuking several of His Apostles when they want to inflict violence on others:

"As the time drew near for him to be taken up to Heaven, Jesus resolutely took the road to Jerusalem and sent messengers ahead of him. These set out, and they went into a Samaritan village to make preparations for him, but the people would not receive him because he was making for Jerusalem. Seeing this, the disciples James and John said, 'Lord, do you want us to call down fire from Heaven to burn them up?' . . . . But he turned and rebuked them, and they went off to another village." (Luke 9:52-56)

The Figurative Use of "Sword" in Christianity

The term "sword" is often used metaphorically in Christian texts. For example, when Simeon prophesied about Mary and Jesus in the Temple:

[He will be] "A light for revelation to the Gentiles, and the glory of your people Israel…. He is destined to be a sign that is rejected and a sword will pierce your own soul too." (Luke 2:32-35)

Simeon is also echoing the words of the prophet Isaiah (Shaya) who proclaimed, "I will make you the light of the nations."

Simeon's insight into Mary's future suffering is recalled by the Damascene in his Homily II on the Assumption:

"It was fitting that she, who had seen her Son upon the Cross and who had thereby received into her heart the sword of sorrow which she had escaped in the act of giving birth to Him, should look upon Him as He sits with the Father."

The figurative use of 'sword' is also used by Isaiah who says God, "made my mouth a sharp sword," and by Saint Paul when he says, "And take the helmet of salvation, and the sword of the Spirit, which is the word of God." (Eph 6:17)

On the other hand, Islam claims the word of God (the Qur'an) came down on Muhammed demanding Islam put on the helmet of salvation by striking a bargain with God, take up the sword and fight Allah's enemies, kill or be killed.

The metaphorical use of the "sword" in Christianity reflects a spiritual battle, not a physical campaign. The true Christian struggle is internal, against sin, falsehood, and the powers of darkness, it is not a call to arms against human opponents. The Word of God is the sword, and it cuts not flesh but hearts (Hebrews 4:12). Christ's kingdom is "not of this world" (John 18:36), and therefore His followers see warfare as a spiritual battle.

Conclusion

As Islam expanded through conquest, it reshaped not only the political landscape but also the religious beliefs of entire nations. The simple faith formula of Islam; the Five Pillars of Faith, Prayer, Almsgiving, Fasting, and Pilgrimage, offered an accessible path that attracted many. Yet, the vine of Jesse (a biblical symbol of God's enduring covenant) continued to flourish in the hearts of believers, even as Islamic influence redefined cultures and challenged Christian teachings moving ever outward from Arabia saying: "They fight in the cause of Allah, so they kill and are killed. [It is] a true promise [binding] upon Him in the Torah and the Gospel and the Qur'an.

CHAPTER 3:
FAULT LINES OF FAITH

The Spread of Islam

The capture of Damascus and Jerusalem paved the way for Islam's expansion into Africa. Alexandria, Egypt's primary port, was the first African city to face Islamic aggression. Initially, the Egyptians sought to avoid invasion by paying the Arabs an annual tribute in gold. However, after three years, they ceased payments, prompting the Arab leader Amr b. al-As to invade.

At the time, Egypt was divided into multiple provinces, each governed independently, leading to a fragmented defence. In 639, Muslim troops invaded the Nile Delta and marched toward Alexandria. Along the way, they massacred the inhabitants of Nikiou, an undefended town. John, the Monophysite Christian bishop of Nikiou, recorded:

"Then the Muslims arrived in Nikiou. There was not one single soldier to resist them. They seized the town and slaughtered everyone they met in the streets and in the churches—men, women, and children, sparing nobody."[20]

Alexandria quickly surrendered rather than resist. Four years later, a Byzantine fleet temporarily recaptured the city, but it soon fell again to the Muslims. According to historian Philip Hitti, a message was sent to Mecca announcing Alexandria's reconquest, with the spoils including 40,000 protection-tax-paying Jews.[21]

Following the fall of Alexandria, Islam expanded westward across North Africa and into Spain. In 711, a Muslim army entered Spain under the pretext of aiding an ally but soon decided to conquer the territory. After a decisive victory at the Battle of Guadalete, the Muslims rapidly occupied most of Spain, completing their conquest within seven years.

Once in control, they systematically eradicated Christian symbols. Islamic teachings prohibit artistic representations of God or holy figures, considering them idolatrous. Historian Darío Fernández-Morera, in *The Myth of the Andalusian Paradise*, describes the destruction of Christian symbols and churches as a standard feature of Islamic conquest. He cites several Muslim historians to support this claim. For instance, in *The History of the Mohammedan Dynasties in Spain*, Al-Maqqari writes that all the churches in and around Córdoba "were immediately pulled down and destroyed."[22]

The last remaining church in Córdoba, the ancient Basilica of Saint Vincent, was sold under duress to the Muslim leader Abd al-Rahman. He demolished most of the church and built the famous Mosque of Córdoba on its site. Though the mosque could have been constructed elsewhere, placing it atop Córdoba's last remaining church symbolized Islam's dominance.

Fernández-Morera also references Al-Razi, another early historian of Islamic Spain, who documented the rulers' efforts to erase Christian heritage:

"He would take all the bodies which Christians honour and call saints and burn them; and he would burn their beautiful churches. In Spain, there were many magnificent churches, some built by the Greeks and some by the Romans. Seeing this, the Christians, when they could, would take their sacred things and flee to the mountains."

This systematic dismantling of churches and veneration sites was not merely an act of conquest but a deliberate effort to erase Christian presence and assert Islamic religious and political authority over the newly acquired territories.

Following their rapid conquest of Spain, Muslim armies pushed further into Europe, crossing the Pyrenees to challenge the Frankish kingdoms of southern France.

Islam Moves into France

Eight years after invading Spain, Muslim forces advanced into southern France. Narbonne fell, and a mosque was established inside the Church of Sainte-Rustique. Using Narbonne as a base, the invaders continued their incursions, forcing many local towns to surrender without resistance. The advance was temporarily halted in 721 when Duke Eudes of Aquitaine won a crucial battle at Toulouse. However, a renewed Muslim offensive in 732 overwhelmed Eudes' forces at Bordeaux, which was sacked and plundered.

France seemed on the brink of collapse when Charles Martel, a Frankish leader, led his army south to confront the invaders near Tours and Poitiers. The Muslims delayed their attack, waiting for their raiding parties to return, allowing Martel to select a favourable battlefield. He positioned his troops on high ground with a forest on one side, shielding them from Muslim cavalry. He also employed a defensive formation similar to the Roman phalanx, with tightly packed spearmen forming an impenetrable wall.

The chronicler Isidore of Beja recorded the battle:

"And in the shock of the battle, the men of the North seemed like a North Sea that cannot be moved. Firmly they stood, one close to another, forming as it were a bulwark of ice; and with great blows of their swords, they hewed down the Arabs. Drawn up in a band around their chief, the people of the Austrasians [modern northeastern France] carried all before them."[23]

Although this battle did not immediately end the Muslim incursions into Aquitaine, it marked the turning point of Islamic expansion into Western Europe. Martel's son, Pepin, pushed the Muslims back into Spain by capturing their base at Narbonne in 759. Later, his grandson, Charlemagne, founded the Spanish March, a buffer zone between his empire and the Muslim-controlled Al-Andalus (Islamic Spain).

The Islamic conquests reshaped the Mediterranean world, spreading their influence across Africa and Europe. Yet, determined resistance from European leaders like Charles Martel and Charlemagne ultimately stemmed the tide, preserving the Christian identity of Western Europe.

While the Frankish realms fortified their borders and pushed back Islamic advances in the West, the Mediterranean's southern shores faced a different but no less fierce challenge.

First Constantinople, Then Rome

While Christian France fought to stem Islamic imperialism, Italy also faced repeated Muslim aggression. In 652 Muslim forces attacked Sicily. Philip Hitti described the impact:

"The delights of Syracuse, ravaged in this first attempt, consisted of women, church treasures, and other valuable booty which invited repeated returns by Muslim plunderers in the second half of the Seventh Century."[24]

A full-scale invasion of Sicily began in 827, and the island soon became a launching point for attacks on mainland Italy. Rome itself was targeted in 846 when a Muslim fleet landed at Ostia, the city's port. Although the invaders failed to breach Rome's walls, they desecrated the tombs of the Popes and looted Saint Peter's Basilica. They also plundered St. Paul's Basilica, built on the site where Christians believe Saint Paul was martyred.

Though Rome survived these early raids, the Islamic threat to the heart of Christendom persisted for centuries, culminating in the fall of Constantinople in 1453.

The greatest threat to Italy arose when Mehmet II captured Constantinople, making his first step towards uniting the old Roman Empire under Islamic rule. Previous Muslim leaders had attempted to conquer the city, but its formidable defences had held firm. Mehmet's decisive strike, however, succeeded where others had failed.

The great cathedral of Hagia Sophia was looted, its precious materials taken, valuable icons destroyed, and all Christian symbols defaced. The cathedral was then converted into a mosque, symbolizing the Islamic conquest of the city. With Constantinople under his control, Mehmet turned his gaze toward Rome.

In 1480, Mehmet's forces, numbering about 18,000 men, landed near Otranto, a coastal town in southern Italy. After a two-week siege, Otranto fell, and the invaders ruthlessly plundered the town. Archbishop Pendinelli was assassinated for refusing to convert to Islam, and his cathedral was stripped of Christian symbols and turned into a stable for horses. All men over the age of 50 were executed, while women and children under 15 were either killed or enslaved. The 800 surviving Christian soldiers were given a choice; convert to Islam or face death. When they refused, they were taken to the Hill of Minerva and slaughtered, their remains later enshrined in glass cases in a side chapel of Otranto Cathedral as a testament to their faith.

Otranto Cathedral. Photo by Keiron Long.

The invaders continued their assaults on Lecce, Taranto, and Brindisi, but as winter approached, Mehmet left a garrison behind and returned to Turkey, preparing for a renewed push into Italy the following year. However, fate intervened because Mehmet died the next year, and with him, his grand plan to conquer Rome. His successor redirected efforts northward, targeting lands beyond Greece.

Centuries earlier, Hannibal of Carthage had invaded northern Italy, aiming to crush Rome and become the dominant power in the Mediterranean. Mehmet's capture of Constantinople and his bloody victory at Otranto positioned him as a new Hannibal, an Islamic crusader seeking to bring Rome to its knees.

Mehmet's shadow loomed large over Europe, but the Islamic threat did not end with his campaigns. Centuries later, the siege of Malta in 1565 once again brought the clash between Christian Europe and Muslim forces to a head.

In May 1565 a Muslim fleet besieged Malta, an island south of Sicily. The siege struck fear into Europe, prompting Queen Elizabeth I of England to express her concerns: "If the Turks should prevail against the Isle of Malta, it is uncertain what further peril might follow to the rest of Christendom."

At the heart of Malta's defence stood the Knights of Malta, an order with a rich history deeply intertwined with the religious and military struggles of Christendom.

Expecting an attack, the Knights of Malta had heavily fortified the island. Fort St. Elmo fell in June after fierce resistance, but the defenders at Forts St. Michael and St. Angelo held their ground. By September, news arrived that a Spanish fleet was on its way, and the demoralized Turks retreated.

The Knights of Malta

The Knights of Malta, originally known as the Order of St. John of Jerusalem, were founded in 1048 by Benedictine Brother Gerard to care for sick pilgrims in the Hospital of St. John in Jerusalem. Over time, the Order developed a military arm to protect its hospitals and Christian travellers. Driven from Jerusalem, the knights relocated to Rhodes, only to be expelled by Suleiman the Magnificent in 1522. In 1530, Charles V of Spain granted them tenure over Malta in exchange for a symbolic gift; a Maltese falcon and a Mass in his honour.

Eventually, the Order left Malta when Napoleon threatened to invade the island on his way to Egypt. Not wishing to fight against a Christian power, the Knights abandoned their fortress and sailed away, eventually making Rome their headquarters, and laying aside their military role and focusing on their charitable and medical mission of caring for the poor and the sick.

Though the Order of Malta repelled one siege, the Ottoman Empire continued its push into Europe, advancing into the Balkans and Central Europe with formidable force.

Islam's Advance into Europe and Beyond

After the fall of Constantinople, Athens soon followed, with resistance proving futile. Muslim forces expanded into Bulgaria, Serbia, Croatia, Montenegro, Macedonia, Romania, and much of Hungary, only halting at the walls of Vienna.

In 1529, Suleiman the Magnificent besieged Vienna, boasting that within two weeks, he would be eating breakfast inside St. Stephen's Cathedral. Two weeks later, the city's defenders mockingly sent word; his breakfast was getting cold. Ultimately, Vienna's resolute defence, aided by unfavourable weather, forced the Sultan's retreat.

Another Muslim siege of Vienna in 1683 was thwarted by Polish King Jan Sobieski III, who led a surprise cavalry charge from the forests above the city. His elite mounted troops, the Winged Hussars, routed the Ottoman forces, securing Vienna and halting the Islamic advance into Central Europe.

Centuries of Ottoman dominance over parts of Southeastern Europe met with persistent resistance, culminating in the Greek War of Independence in the early 19th century.

The Greek Struggle for Independence

Unlike Vienna, Athens endured centuries of Ottoman rule before regaining its freedom. The Greek War of Independence began in the 1820s, culminating in victory by 1829. The Treaty of Adrianople, an agreement between Russia and the Ottoman Empire, granted Greece autonomy, marking a significant turning point in its struggle.

One of the war's heroes was Konstantinos Kanaris, a naval captain who avenged the 1822 Chios massacre by launching a fireship attack on the Muslim leader responsible. The massacre had seen Ottoman troops slaughter infants, males over 12, and females over 40, sparing only those who converted to Islam. The war's brutalities reflected the deep religious and cultural divisions of the time.

Konstantinos Kanaris, a member of the Greek resistance. Collection of Greek Parliament / Wikimedia Commons.

Clash of Faiths

Throughout history, the expansion of Islam brought it into confrontation with diverse religious communities, from the heartlands of Christendom to the temples of India. These encounters shaped empires, divided peoples, and left legacies that still echo today.

Beyond the military and political advances into Europe and the Mediterranean, Islam's expansion brought it into contact with diverse religious communities across Asia and Africa, many of which faced severe challenges under its rule.

As Islam expanded beyond Europe, its treatment of non-Muslims was often severe. Hindus and Buddhists, deemed idolaters, faced harsh persecution. By the time Islam reached India, its power was such that it viewed other faiths with contempt.

A Pakistani scholar echoed these sentiments in *Demons from the Past*, published in the Pakistan Daily Times in August 2004 observing:

"While historical events should be judged in the context of their times, it cannot be denied that even in that bloody period of history, no mercy was shown to the Hindus unfortunate enough to be in the path of either the Arab conquerors of Sindh and south Punjab, or the Central Asians who swept in from Afghanistan… Their temples were razed, their idols smashed, their women raped, their men killed or taken slaves. When Mahmud of Ghazni entered Somnath on one of his annual raids, he slaughtered all 50,000 inhabitants. These conquerors justified their deeds by claiming it was their religious duty to smite non-believers. Cloaking themselves in the banner of Islam, they claimed they were fighting for their faith when, in reality, they were indulging in straightforward slaughter and pillage."

While some may seek to understand these actions within their historical context, the scale and brutality of the campaigns against non-Muslim communities remain undeniable. This view is echoed by historian Will Durant, who described the Islamic conquest of India as one of history's bloodiest episodes.

To this day, large regions of Africa, the Middle East, and parts of Asia remain dominated by Islam. It is a faith that asserts God has no associates, despite humanity being made in His image. The expansion of Islam reshaped the political and religious landscape of vast territories, leaving a lasting impact on history. From the conquest of Constantinople to the sieges of Vienna and the wars in India, the spread of Islam was marked by both military triumphs and the suppression of other faiths. The echoes of these conflicts continue to influence global relations today.

Beyond its outward expansion and interactions with other faiths, Islam has also been marked by deep internal divisions, most notably, the split between Sunni and Shia Muslims.

Sunni versus Shia

The term *Shia* comes from *Shia'tu Ali*, meaning *the party of Ali* or *supporters of Ali*. Shia Muslims believe that Ali ibn Abi Talib, Muhammad's cousin and son-in-law, was the rightful leader of the Muslim community. Ali was married to Muhammad's daughter, Fatima, and Shia doctrine holds that leadership (the Imamate) should remain within the Prophet's family, passing through Ali and his descendants.

In contrast, *Sunni* comes from *Ahl al-Sunnah wa'l-Jama'ah*, meaning *the people of the tradition and the community*. Sunni Muslims argue that leadership should be determined by consensus rather than bloodline, relying on religious scholars (ulama) for guidance. Sunni doctrine is based on the Qur'an, the Hadith (sayings and actions of the Prophet), and scholarly consensus (ijma).

Sunni Muslims recognize the first four caliphs; Abu Bakr, Umar, Uthman, and Ali, as Muhammad's rightful successors. Shia Muslims, however, reject the legitimacy of the first three caliphs and consider Ali to be the first divinely appointed Imam. Unlike Sunnis, Shia Islam follows a hierarchy of religious clerics, with figures such as Ayatollahs holding significant authority. Shia theology also includes the belief in infallible Imams, divinely guided leaders who are seen as the true heirs of Muhammad's spiritual and political authority.

This theological and political rift has profoundly influenced Muslim history, shaping the development of communities, governance, and religious authority up to the present day. Today, Iran stands as the foremost Shia-majority nation, highlighting the ongoing religious and political significance of this divide.

Ali's rule (656–661 AD) was marred by civil strife and ended with his assassination in 661 AD. His eldest son, Hassan, faced intense pressure to relinquish his claim to the caliphate, while his younger son, Hussein, departed Mecca in 680 to lead a revolt against the Umayyad Caliphate. Hussein was intercepted by Umayyad forces near the Euphrates River, where, at the Battle of Karbala, he and his supporters were defeated. His severed head was sent to the Umayyad ruler Yazid in Damascus. This tragic event became a defining moment in Shia history, with Hussein and his followers revered as martyrs who stood against tyranny.

Shia resentment toward the Umayyads deepened with suspicions that Hassan was poisoned by orders from Caliph Muawiyah. Distrust of Sunni rulers grew further when Ali's later son, Muhammad ibn al-Hanafiyya, openly criticized the Umayyad dynasty, dismissing some of their hadiths as fabrications.

These early events entrenched divisions that have echoed through centuries, fuelling political and religious tensions in the Muslim world today.

Shia Muslims hold that Muhammad designated Ali as his rightful successor, citing hadiths such as one attributed to Zaid ibn al-Arqam, where the Prophet is said to have declared:

"Harken! Allah is my Master and I am the master of the believers." Then he raised Ali's hand and said, "Ali is the master of whoever accepts me as his master. O Lord! Befriend whoever befriends Ali and alienate Yourself from whoever alienates Ali."

Sunnis dispute this interpretation, arguing that the Arabic word mawla (translated as "master") has multiple meanings, such as friend, client, protector, and that this statement does not imply a divine appointment of Ali as Muhammad's successor. Sunni scholars also point to alternative hadiths suggesting Ali himself did not claim an inherited right to lead Islam.

This dispute over leadership is further complicated by ongoing debates among scholars regarding the authenticity and political motivations behind various hadith collections.

Islam and Culture

Amid the turbulence of theological conflict and political upheaval, Islamic civilization also produced notable intellectual and cultural achievements. It is often claimed, especially in modern academic circles, that the West owes much of its intellectual heritage to Islamic civilization. However, this narrative is far from straightforward and deserves careful examination.

The claim that Western civilization owes a great debt to Islamic learning likely traces back to the Abbasid dynasty. During this period, particularly under Caliph al-Mansur, who established the city of Baghdad between 762 and 764, and his successor Al-Mamun, significant intellectual advancements took place. Al-Mamun founded the renowned House of Wisdom in Baghdad, where Greek, Indian, Roman, and Persian texts were translated into Arabic and made accessible to scholars. This institution facilitated Arab progress in various fields of science and culture. For instance, the Islamic physician Abu Bakr Muhammad ibn Zakariyya al-Razi built upon the work of Galen, contributing significantly to medical knowledge with his texts *On Surgery* and *A General Book on Therapy*.

Some Islamic historians present a narrative suggesting Europe was intellectually stagnant during the Middle Ages while learning flourished exclusively in the Arab world. Philip Hitti, for example, asserts:

"All this took place while Europe was almost totally ignorant of Greek thought and science. For while al-Mamun was delving into Greek and Persian philosophy, their contemporaries in the West, Charlemagne and his lords, were reportedly dabbling in the art of writing their names."[25]

This argument, however, is overly simplistic. While parts of Europe faced challenges due to invasions and political fragmentation, intellectual life persisted in monasteries, courts, and emerging universities. Charlemagne himself was far from unlearned. Einhard, his private secretary, provides a different perspective in The Life of Charlemagne:

"He also gave attention to the liberal arts, and had great respect for those who taught them, for grammar, especially, he learned from Peter of Pisa, a deacon of his old age. Another deacon, Alcuin, a Saxon from Britain, of the school of York, was his teacher in other subjects. Under his guidance, the King spent much time in learning rhetoric, dialectics, and particularly astronomy. He learned to compute and with deep interest and curiosity, he investigated the motions of the stars. He tried to write, and used to keep tablets under his pillow to practice forming letters in his leisure hours, but he made little progress because he had not taken up the study in his early years."[26]

Einhard's account illustrates that medieval Europe fostered learning in various intellectual centres, particularly in courts and monasteries. Charlemagne himself encouraged education and engaged with leading scholars of his time.

The narrative that the Arab world was uniquely responsible for preserving and advancing knowledge overlooks the fact that the intellectual flowering of the Islamic world was built on the scholarship of the Greeks, Persians, Syrians, and

Indians, incorporated into the expanding Muslim empire. The Arabs themselves had not shown much scholarly interest before their conquests brought them into contact with these advanced civilizations.

Thus, while Al-Mamun's House of Wisdom played a key role in preserving and disseminating knowledge because it enabled the Islamic world to catch up to and build upon the broader civilized world's traditions.

Ultimately, learning and culture were always present in Europe, though their expression varied due to external pressures such as barbarian invasions and Muslim incursions. Knowledge was preserved and cultivated in various European institutions, ensuring intellectual progress continued throughout the Middle Ages.

Yet cultural achievement cannot substitute for theological truth. No matter how refined a civilization's art, science, or literature may be, it ultimately stands or falls on the view it holds of God. And here again, Islam diverges dramatically from Christian doctrine, especially in its rejection of the Trinity and the divine Sonship of Christ. To better understand this divergence, we must revisit an earlier controversy that shaped the Church's own understanding of who Jesus truly is: the Arian heresy.

Arius and the Trinity

A friend mused that, "from the beginning of the Church, new Christians were baptised 'in the name of the Father and of the Son and of the Holy Spirit.' There is one name because there is one God. Arius caused the greatest problem for the Church after New Testament times. Arius and his followers would say all the words of the New Testament, but they would interpret them in their own way. They could not get beyond the world of the imagination; they thought that the Father must be older than the Son, the Son must be created, the greatest of creatures.

"...the only-begotten, begotten of the Father before all ages; Light from Light; true God from true God; begotten, not made; of one essence with the Father, by whom all things were made."

We can understand more deeply what this means by turning to the writings of St. Irenaeus and St. Thomas Aquinas."

Saint Thomas Aquinas (1225–1274) challenged the Arian belief that Christ was a created being, subordinate to the Father not only in His human nature but also in His divine nature. According to Aquinas, Arius and his followers misunderstood Christ's nature by choosing their own interpretations over the teachings handed down by Christ.

Aquinas specifically challenged Arius's interpretation of Jesus' words, "I came forth," arguing that Arius incorrectly understands this phrase as implying Christ came forth as an effect from a cause. Aquinas instead asserts that Christ's coming forth should be understood as an interior activity, similar to knowledge that remains within the knower. Since God is pure mind and pure act, His understanding is identical to His being, and His knowledge is the cause of creation.

Saint Irenaeus, offers a similar perspective on the Trinity aligning with Aquinas's explanation of the divine interior activity. He describes the Trinity as follows:

"So, then, there is one God, the Father, uncreated, invisible, creator of all things. There is no other God above Him and no other God beneath Him. God is rational, and therefore produces by His Reason—Word. God is also Spirit, and so He ordered all things by the Spirit, as the prophet says: 'By the word of the Lord the Heavens were established, and all the powers of them by His Spirit' (Psalm 32).

The Word 'establishes'—that is, produces bodies and bestows permanence on what has come into existence, while the Spirit disposes and shapes the various 'powers.' The Word is rightly called the Son, and the Spirit is God's Wisdom. The apostle Paul puts it well: 'One God and Father of all, who is above all and with all and in all' (Ephesians 4:6). The Father is 'above all,' but the Word is 'with all,' since it is through Him that everything was made by the Father. And 'in us all' is the Spirit, who cries 'Abba, Father' (Galatians 4:6) and forms man into the likeness of God. The Spirit manifests the Word, and so the prophets proclaim the Son of God. But the Word lets the Spirit blow, and so it is He who speaks in the prophets and leads men back to the Father."[27]

Both Aquinas and Irenaeus emphasize that the Trinity is an essential unity, with the Father, Son, and Holy Spirit operating in perfect harmony rather than as separate beings in a hierarchical structure.

in Summa Theologica (especially in Part I, Q. 27), Thomas Aquinas explains that the only processions in God are those that arise from immanent (internal) acts rather than transient (external) ones. He identifies two such processions:

The Procession of the Word (or Son) – This corresponds to God's act of understanding. God's perfect self-knowledge generates the Divine Word (Logos), which is the Son.

The Procession of Love (or Spirit) – This corresponds to God's act of willing or loving. The love that proceeds from God's perfect self-knowledge is the Holy Spirit.

Aquinas argues that these processions are unique because they remain within God, unlike creation, which is an external act. This distinction is essential in Trinitarian theology: the Son proceeds by way of intellect (Word), and the Spirit proceeds by way of will (Love).

Since the Spirit is the bond of love between the Father and Son, it is fitting to say the Spirit proceeds from both. When Jesus breathes on the disciples and says, "Receive the Holy Spirit" (John 20:22) He shows the Spirit proceeding from the Son, reminding us that the Spirit is also associated with the His divine mission.

Saying the Spirit proceeds from both the Father and the Son also expresses the perfect unity and co-equality of the three divine persons.

Arius's argument that, "there was a time when the Son was not," was refuted by the Church Fathers. They affirmed that Christ is not a created being but eternally begotten, sharing in the divine essence of the Father. This understanding of the Trinity, that God is one in essence but three in persons, preserved both the unity and distinction within the Godhead. Arianism was rejected as a heresy. The controversy ultimately reinforced the doctrine of the Trinity as a central Christian belief.

If Arius denied Christ's divinity, Islam echoes that denial, making it not a new revelation, but a repetition of an ancient error.

Islam also claimed that Muhammed was God's final messenger. Is this true?

Miracle of the Sun / Wikimedia Commons.

Messengers from Heaven

Although Muhammad declared himself to be the last and greatest of God's messengers, yet history records many instances where individuals have acted as divine messengers since his time. One such example is the extraordinary events that unfolded in 1917 in a small village near Fatima, Portugal, where three children reported a series of visions that would become one of the most significant Marian apparitions in history.

Why Fatima? A Historical and Spiritual Connection

Why did Mary choose to visit an area as seemingly insignificant as Fatima? The answer may be found in Portugal's history, beginning with a legend and culminating in the deep devotion of the Portuguese nobility to Mary.

A legend, dating back to 1158, tells of a Muslim princess from Alcácer do Sal who fell in love with a Portuguese knight, Gonçalo Hermingues. She converted to Christianity, taking the name Oureana, yet she was originally called Fatima. After her untimely death, Gonçalo entered monastic life, burying her remains near his monastery in the mountains. Over time, the surrounding area became known as Fatima.

Another possibility is that the village was named in honour of Muhammad's daughter, Fatima, a revered figure in Islamic tradition.

However, a third and more spiritually significant reason for Mary's visits may lie in Portugal's long-standing veneration of Mary. After securing independence from Spain in 1385, King John I built a church in her honour. Three years later, he commissioned the grand Santa Maria de Vitória, where he was later buried alongside his wife, Philippa of Lancaster, and their son, Prince Henry the Navigator.

In 1646, King John IV declared Mary the Patroness of Portugal under the title of the Immaculate Conception, even placing his crown at her statue's feet as a sign of Portugal's devotion. This belief, that Mary was conceived without original sin, was widely accepted long before it became official Catholic doctrine.

Could this profound national devotion have led Mary to return their love by appearing in Fatima, offering strength to the faithful at a time when the anti-Catholic, Masonic-led government sought to suppress the Church? The supporters of the ruling authorities had burned down over 100 churches, persecuted clergy, banned religious schools, and even abolished church feast days; renaming Christmas as "Family Feast Day."

The Apparitions of Fatima

In 1917, three shepherd children, Lucia dos Santos and her cousins Francisco and Jacinta Marto, received a series of heavenly visitations. An angel first appeared to them, announcing that Mary would soon come. When she did, she called for prayer and penance to help end the First World War, and to prevent the next.

On October 13, 1917, before a crowd of 70,000 people, including atheists and sceptics, the famous Miracle of the Sun occurred. Witnesses reported seeing the sun "dance" in the sky, changing colours and appearing to plunge toward the earth before returning to its place. This phenomenon was reminiscent of the biblical sign given to King Hezekiah when God made the sun's shadow move backward ten steps (2 Kings 20:8-11).

Messages and Warnings from Heaven

During her apparitions, Mary issued warnings about the coming Russian Revolution and the spread of atheistic communism. She also spoke of moral decay, lamenting that many would abandon marriage and live in sin. She specifically warned that most souls who perish are lost due to sins of impurity.

Mary also told Jacinta of her sorrow over offenses against God and lamented the many sins of the flesh and certain modern fashions that she said were displeasing to Him.

Saint Paul's Letter to the Galatians describes "sins of the flesh" as:

"Sexual immorality, impurity and debauchery; idolatry and witchcraft; hatred, discord, jealousy, fits of rage, selfish ambition, dissensions, factions and envy; drunkenness, orgies, and the like. I warn you, as I did before, that those who live like this will not inherit the kingdom of God." (Galatians 5:19-21)

The Book of Wisdom puts it more philosophically:

"For the fascination of evil throws good things into the shade, and the whirlwind of desire corrupts a simple heart." (Wisdom 4:12)

Jacinta died in 1920, but when her tomb was opened in 1935, her body was found to be incorrupt; a phenomenon often associated with sainthood. Her remains were transferred to Fatima, where she was laid to rest beside her brother Francisco.

Prophecies of War and Persecution

Mary also warned that if people did not turn back to God, another war would follow. She specified that it would begin during the reign of Pope Pius XI (1922–1939). True to her prophecy, in 1936, communist forces in Spain, calling themselves "Republicans," sought to transform the country into a socialist state.

Historian Rodney Stark, in his book, *Bearing False Witness*,[28] records that this movement resulted in the brutal murder of:

13 bishops
4,172 priests and seminarians
2,364 monks and friars
283 nuns

This attack on religion triggered a military intervention by General Francisco Franco, sparking the Spanish Civil War.

Mary's Five Sorrows

In 1925, Mary revealed to Lucia that five types of blasphemies deeply wounded her heart:

Blasphemies against her Immaculate Conception
Blasphemies against her virginity
Blasphemies against her divine maternity
Blasphemies of those who foster hatred or indifference toward her
Blasphemies of those who defile her sacred images

Other Apparitions Throughout History

Mary's presence in Fatima is part of a broader pattern of divine messages sent throughout history. Other significant Marian apparitions and heavenly visitations include:

Guadalupe, Mexico (1531)
Paris, France (1830) – The Miraculous Medal
La Salette, France (1846)
Lourdes, France (1858)
Christ's appearances to St. Faustina in Poland (1931)
Padre Pio's mystical experiences in Italy (until his death in 1968)
Akita, Japan (1973)
Kibeho, Rwanda (1981)

Despite their historical significance, such events receive little attention in secular society, which often views the world through the lens of natural selection and evolution rather than divine intervention.

One of the most profound Marian apparitions occurred in Paris in 1830 when Mary appeared to St. Catherine Laboure, instructing her to create the Miraculous Medal. This medal depicted two hearts, one surrounded by a crown of thorns and the other pierced by a sword. The inscription read:

"Mary, conceived without sin, pray for us who have recourse to you."

Perhaps this message influenced Pope Blessed Pius IX's to declare in 1854 that the Immaculate Conception was an official Church dogma.

When divine messages are reported, Church authorities conduct investigations, often leading to official declarations of credibility or scepticism. Ultimately, belief in private revelations is left to the individual. However, the events mentioned above were all deemed worthy of belief by the Church. The events at Fatima and other approved apparitions demonstrate that God remains active in His creation, continuing to call humanity to conversion, penance, and prayer, and these things have the power to change the course of history.

Icons

What a messenger reveals about God shapes how God is to be worshipped. And that includes how He is depicted, or not depicted. The Christian use of icons has long been a point of contention, not only within Christendom but especially in dialogue with Islam, which denounces any visual representation of the divine. Yet this difference is not merely stylistic, it reflects a deeper divide in how each faith understands incarnation, beauty, and presence.

Sister Lucia, one of the seers of Fatima, put forward a simple but accurate understanding of the role of art in religious practise. In *"Calls" From the Message of Fatima*, she says:

"God commands us to adore Him alone, because He alone is to be adored by His creatures. He forbids us to make idols out of the things that were created by Him and which are even more powerless than we are: they can do nothing and are worth nothing, which is why He forbids us to pay homage to them, or to adore them.

But we must distinguish between the idols to which God refers in this commandment and the images of Christ, Our Lady and the Saints. We do not, nor should we adore any of these images. We venerate them on account of what they represent and recall to our minds, in the same way as we venerate pictures of our parents, our brothers and sisters or our friends, placing them in the most honoured places in our homes so that we can see them better, and also so that the people who visit us can see them and be reminded of them too. We venerate the images of Jesus Christ, of Our Lady and of the Saints because they remind us of the people that they represent, of their virtues and of their teaching, and so encourage us to follow their example."

A VENERABLE ICON

An example of an icon worthy of veneration is the picture of Mary of Guadalupe which traces back to 1531 when Mary appeared to a Mexican named Juan Diego. She asked him to tell the bishop to build a church on the hill where they were standing. Mary told Juan to take some roses from nearby and carry them to the bishop in his tilba, a cloak woven from cactus leaves. When the roses fell to the ground in front of the bishop an image of the woman Juan had been talking to, appeared on the inside of the tilba. The image hangs in the Basilica of Our Lady of Guadalupe, Mexico City. The image isn't painted and scientists can't work out how it was made.

Our Lady of Guadalupe, Mexico, 1531 / Wikimedia Commons.

SAINT JOHN OF DAMASCUS AND THE VENERATION OF ICONS

At the heart of the Christian defence of icons stands a voice uniquely placed to understand both sides, St. John of Damascus. Living under Islamic rule, the Damascene witnessed firsthand the rise of Islamic iconoclasm and responded not with rebellion, but with theological clarity. In defending icons, he wasn't just defending art, he was defending the Incarnation, God becoming human in the form of Jesus.

The Damascene was a strong advocate for the veneration of icons, particularly in response to the iconoclastic policies of Emperor Leo III of Constantinople. In 726 and 730, Leo, assuming both the roles of Emperor and Patriarch, ordered the removal of all religious images from churches and homes within his domain. This policy may have been influenced by the growing Muslim presence on Byzantine borders, as in 721, Caliph Yazid had similarly banned holy images from all Christian churches within his realm.

The Damascene lamented the destruction of religious art, arguing that images serve as vital memorials, akin to the role of words for those who hear. He famously stated:

"The image is a memorial, just what words are to a listening ear."

He also criticized the apparent inconsistency in Islamic practices, pointing out the veneration of the Kaaba in Mecca:

"And we answer them: 'How is it, then, that you rub yourselves against a stone in your Ka'ba and kiss and embrace it?'"

Despite the political, economic, and religious pressures that led many to accept the destruction of icons, John of Damascus remained steadfast in his defence of religious imagery. Unlike others who may have been swayed by patronage or material gain, he refused to compromise his beliefs. His theological writings provided a robust defence of icon veneration, arguing that religious images serve as a means to honour, rather than worship, the divine.

John of Damascus played a crucial role in preserving the tradition of icon veneration in Christian worship. His writings not only opposed the iconoclastic policies of Emperor Leo III but also provided a theological foundation for the continued use of religious images in the Church. By emphasizing that icons serve as visual reminders of the divine, rather than objects of worship, he reinforced the idea that sacred art is an essential part of Christian devotion. His unwavering stance ensured that the veneration of icons would endure despite political and religious opposition.

Conclusion

The Damascene highlighted the differences between Christianity and Islam are not just paintings of the divine from different perspectives; they are anchored in fundamentally different images of God, of revelation, and of salvation. One paints a picture of a God who enters history, takes on flesh, and redeems His creation through sacrificial love. The other paints over and blots out the incarnation, the crucifixion, and the Trinity and offers instead a distant God, a final prophet, and a book that contradicts the Gospel while claiming to confirm it.

Christians cannot ignore these contradictions. Even though Islam offers a Five Pillar pathway to God, it does not recognize the profound theological claim at the heart of the Christian faith; that in Jesus Christ, the fullness of God was pleased to dwell (Colossians 1:19), and that there is no other name under heaven given among men by which we must be saved (Acts 4:12).

In the end, the question is not merely historical or doctrinal, it is eternal. Did God speak once in Christ, or must we wait for another word? If the answer is Christ, then every other claim, however noble or devout, must bow before Him.

Apologia by St John of Damascus (The Defence of Icons)

"WITH the ever-present conviction of my own unworthiness, I ought to have kept silence and confessed my shortcomings before God, but all things are good at the right time. I see the Church which God founded on the Apostles and Prophets, its corner-stone being Christ His Son, tossed on an angry sea, beaten by rushing waves, shaken and troubled by the assaults of evil spirits. I see rents in the seamless robe of Christ, which impious men have sought to part asunder, and His body cut into pieces, that is, the word of God and the ancient tradition of the Church. Therefore, I have judged it unreasonable to keep silence and to hold my tongue, bearing in mind the Scripture warning: "If thou withdrawest thyself, my soul shall not delight in thee," (Hebrew 10:38) and "If thou seest the sword coming and dost not warn thy brother, I shall require his blood at thy hand." (cf. Ezekiel. 33:8) Fear, then, compelled me to speak; the truth was stronger than the majesty of kings. "I bore testimony to Thee before kings," I heard the royal David saying, "and I

was not ashamed." (Psalm 119:46) No, I was the more incited to speak. The King's command is all powerful over his subjects. For few men have hitherto been found who, whilst recognising the power of the earthly king to come from above, have resisted his unlawful demands.

In the first place, grasping as a kind of pillar, or foundation, the teaching of the Church, which is our salvation, I have opened out its meaning, giving, as it were, the reins to a well-caparisoned charger. For I look upon it as a great calamity that the Church, adorned with her great privileges and the holiest examples of saints in the past, should go back to the first rudiments, and fear where there is no fear. It is disastrous to suppose that the Church does not know God as He is, that she degenerates into idolatry, for if she declines from perfection in a single iota, it is as an enduring mark on a comely face, destroying by its unsightliness the beauty of the whole. A small thing is not small when it leads to something great, nor indeed is it a thing of no matter to give up the ancient tradition of the Church held by our forefathers, whose conduct we should observe, and whose faith we should imitate.

In the first place, then, before speaking to you, I beseech Almighty God, to whom all things lie open, who knows my small capacity and my genuine intention, to bless the words of my mouth, and to enable me to bridle my mind and direct it to Him, to walk in His presence straightly, not declining to a plausible right hand, nor knowing the left. Then I ask all God's people, the chosen ones of His royal priesthood, with the holy shepherd of Christ's orthodox flock, who represents in his own person Christ's priesthood, to receive my treatise with kindness. They must not dwell on my unworthiness, nor seek for eloquence, for I am only too conscious of my shortcomings. They must consider the thoughts themselves. The Kingdom of

Heaven is not in word but in deed. Conquest is not my object. I raise a hand which is fighting for the truth – a willing hand under the divine guidance.

Relying, then, upon substantial truth as my auxiliary, I will enter on my subject matter. I have taken heed to the words of Truth Himself: "The Lord thy God is one" (Deuteronomy 6:4) and "Thou shalt fear the Lord thy God, and shalt serve Him only, and thou shalt not have strange gods."(Deut. 6:13) Again, "Thou shalt not make to thyself a graven thing, nor the likeness of anything that is in Heaven above, or in the earth beneath" (Exodus 20:4); and "Let them be all confounded that adore graven things." (Ps. 97.7) Again, "The gods that have not made Heaven and earth, let them perish." (Jeremiah 10:11) In this way God spoke of old to the patriarchs through the prophets, and lastly, through His only-begotten Son, on whose account He made the ages. He says, "This is eternal life, that they may know Thee, the only true God, and Jesus Christ whom Thou didst send." (John 17:3)

I believe in one God, the source of all things, without beginning, uncreated, immortal, everlasting, incomprehensible, bodiless, invisible, uncircumscribed, without form. I believe in one supersubstantial being, one divine Godhead in three entities, the Father, the Son, and the Holy Ghost, and I adore Him alone with the worship of latreia [reverence directed only to the Holy Trinity]. I adore one God, one Godhead but three Persons, God the Father, God the Son made flesh, and God the Holy Ghost, one God. I do not adore creation more than the Creator, but I adore the creature created as I am, adopting creation freely and spontaneously that He might elevate our nature and make us partakers of His divine nature. Together with my Lord and King I worship Him clothed in the flesh, not as if it were a garment or He constituted a fourth person of the

Trinity – God forbid. That flesh is divine, and endures after its assumption. Human nature was not lost in the Godhead, but just as the Word made flesh remained the Word, so flesh became the Word remaining flesh, becoming, rather, one with the Word through union. Therefore, I venture to draw an image of the invisible God, not as invisible, but as having become visible for our sakes through flesh and blood. I do not draw an image of the immortal Godhead. I paint the visible flesh of God, for it is impossible to represent a spirit, how much more God who gives breath to the spirit.

Now adversaries say: God's commands to Moses the law-giver were, "Thou shalt adore shalt worship him the Lord thy God, and thou alone, and thou shalt not make to thyself a graven thing that is in Heaven above, or in the earth beneath." They err truly, not knowing the Scriptures, for the letter kills whilst the spirit quickens—not finding in the letter the hidden meaning. I could say to these people, with justice, He who taught you this would teach you the following. Listen to the law-giver's interpretation in Deuteronomy: "And the Lord spoke to you from the midst of the fire. You heard the voice of His words, but you saw not any form at all." (Deut. 4:12) And shortly afterwards: "Keep your souls carefully. You saw not any similitude in the day that the Lord God spoke to you in Horeb from the midst of the fire, lest perhaps being deceived you might make you a graven similitude, or image of male and female, the similitude of any beasts that are upon the earth, or of birds that fly under heaven." (Deut. 4.15-17) And again, "Lest, perhaps, lifting up thy eyes to heaven, thou see the sun and the moon, and all the stars of heaven, and being deceived by error thou adore and serve them." (Deut. 4:19)

You see the one thing to be aimed at is not to adore a created thing more than the Creator, nor to give the worship of latreia *except to Him alone. By worship, consequently, He always understands the worship of latreia. For, again, He says: "Thou shalt not have strange gods other than Me. Thou shalt not make to thyself a graven thing, nor any similitude. Thou shalt not adore them, and thou shalt not serve them, for I am the Lord thy God." (Deut. 5.7–9) And again, "Overthrow their altars, and break down their statues; burn their groves with fire, and break their idols in pieces. For thou shalt not adore a strange god." (Deut. 12.3) And a little further on: "Thou shalt not make to thyself gods of metal." (Ex. 34.17)*

You see that He forbids image-making on account of idolatry, and that it is impossible to make an image of the immeasurable, uncircumscribed, invisible God. You have not seen the likeness of Him, the Scripture says, and this was St Paul's testimony as he stood in the midst of the Areopagus: "Being, therefore, the offspring of God, we must not suppose the divinity to be like unto gold, or silver, or stone, the graving of art, and device of man." (Acts 17.29)

These injunctions were given to the Jews on account of their proneness to idolatry. Now we, on the contrary, are no longer in leading strings. Speaking theologically, it is given to us to avoid superstitious error, to be with God in the knowledge of the truth, to worship God alone, to enjoy the fullness of His knowledge. We have passed the stage of infancy, and reached the perfection of manhood. We receive our habit of mind from God, and know what may be imaged and what may not. The Scripture says, "You have not seen the likeness of Him." (Exodus 33:20) What wisdom in the law-giver. How depict the invisible? How picture the inconceivable? How give expression to the limitless, the immeasurable, the invisible? How give a form to immensity? How paint immortality? How localise mystery?

It is clear that when you contemplate God, who is a pure spirit, becoming man for your sake, you will be able to clothe Him with the human form. When the Invisible One becomes visible to flesh, you may then draw a likeness of His form. When He who is a pure spirit, without form or limit, immeasurable in the boundlessness of His own nature, existing as God, takes upon Himself the form of a servant in substance and in stature, and a body of flesh, then you may draw His likeness, and show it to anyone willing to contemplate it. Depict His ineffable condescension, His virginal birth, His baptism in the Jordan, His transfiguration on Thabor, His all-powerful sufferings, His death and miracles, the proofs of His Godhead, the deeds which He worked in the flesh through divine power, His saving Cross, His Sepulchre, and Resurrection, and ascent into Heaven. Give to it all the endurance of engraving and colour.

Have no fear or anxiety; worship is not all of the same kind. Abraham worshipped the sons of Emmor, impious men in ignorance of God, when he bought the double cave for a tomb. (Genesis 23:7; Acts of the Apostles 7:16) Jacob worshipped his brother Esau and Pharao, the Egyptian, but on the point of his staff. (Gen 33:3) He worshipped, he did not adore. Josue and Daniel worshipped an angel of God (Joshua 5.14) they did not adore him. The worship of latreia is one thing, and the worship which is given to merit another.

Now, as we are talking of images and worship, let us analyse the exact meaning of each. An image is a likeness of the original with a certain difference, for it is not an exact reproduction of the original. Thus, the Son is the living, substantial, unchangeable Image of the invisible God (St Paul's Letter to the Colossians 1:15), bearing in Himself the whole Father, being in all things equal to Him, differing only in being begotten by the Father, who is the Begetter; the Son is begotten.

The Father does not proceed from the Son, but the Son from the Father. It is through the Son, though not after Him, that He is what He is, the Father who generates. In God, too, there are representations and images of His future acts,—that is to say, His counsel from all eternity, which is ever unchangeable. That which is divine is immutable; there is no change in Him, nor shadow of change. (James 1:17) Blessed Denis, who has made divine things in God's presence his study, says that these representations and images are marked out beforehand. In His counsels, God has noted and settled all that He would do, the unchanging future events before they came to pass. In the same way, a man who wished to build a house would first make and think out a plan. Again, visible things are images of invisible and intangible things, on which they throw a faint light. Holy Scripture clothes in figure God and the angels, and the same holy man (Blessed Denis) explains why. When sensible things sufficiently render what is beyond sense, and give a form to what is intangible, a medium would be reckoned imperfect according to our standard, if it did not fully represent material vision, or if it required effort of mind.

If, therefore, Holy Scripture, providing for our need, ever putting before us what is intangible, clothes it in flesh, does it not make an image of what is thus invested with our nature, and brought to the level of our desires, yet invisible? A certain conception through the senses thus takes place in the brain, which was not there before, and is transmitted to the judicial faculty, and added to the mental store. Gregory, who is so eloquent about God, says that the mind, which is set upon getting beyond corporeal things, is incapable of doing it. For the invisible things of God since the creation of the world are made visible through images. (St Paul's Letter to the Romans 1:20) We see images in creation which remind us faintly of God, as when, for instance, we speak of the Holy and Adorable Trinity, imaged by the sun, or light, or burning rays, or by a running fountain, or a full river, or by the mind, speech, or the spirit within us, or by a rose tree, or a sprouting flower, or a sweet fragrance.

Again, an image is expressive of something in the future, mystically shadowing forth what is to happen. For instance, the Ark represents the image of Our Lady, Mother of God, so does the staff and the earthen jar. The serpent brings before us Him who vanquished on the Cross the bite of the original serpent; the sea, water, and the cloud the grace of baptism. (St Paul's First Letter to the Corinthians 10:1)

Again, things which have taken place are expressed by images for the remembrance either of a wonder, or an honour, or dishonour, or good or evil, to help those who look upon it in after times that we may avoid evils and imitate goodness. It is of two kinds, the written image in books, as when God had the law inscribed on tablets, and when He enjoined that the lives of holy men should be recorded and sensible memorials be preserved in remembrance; as, for instance, the earthen jar and the staff in the Ark. (Exodus 34:28; The Letter to the Hebrews 9:4) *So now we preserve in writing the images and the good deeds of the past. Either, therefore, take away images altogether and be out of harmony with God, who made these regulations, or receive them with the language and in the manner which befits them.*

In speaking of the manner let us go into the question of worship. Worship is the symbol of veneration and of honour. Let us understand that there are different degrees of worship. First of all, the worship of latreia, which we show to God, who alone by nature is worthy of worship. When, for the sake of God who is worshipful by nature, we honour His saints and servants, as Josue and Daniel worshipped an angel, and David

His holy places, when he says, "Let us go to the place where His feet have stood." (Ps. 132:7) Again, in His tabernacles, as when all the people of Israel adored in the tent, and standing round the temple in Jerusalem, fixing their gaze upon it from all sides, and worshipping from that day to this, or in the rulers established by Him, as Jacob rendered homage to Esau, his elder brother, (Gen. 33:3) and to Pharaoh, the divinely established ruler. (Gen. 47:7) Joseph was worshipped by his brothers. (Gen. 50.18) I am aware that worship was based on honour, as in the case of Abraham and the sons of Emmor. (Gen. 23.7) Either, then, do away with worship, or receive it altogether according to its proper measure.

Answer me this question. Is there only one God? You answer, "Yes, there is only one Law-giver." Why, then, does He command contrary things? The cherubim are not outside of creation; why, then, does He allow cherubim carved by the hand of man to overshadow the mercy-seat? Is it not evident that – as it is impossible to make an image of God, who is uncircumscribed and impassable, or of one like to God – creation should not be worshipped as God? He allows the image of the cherubim who are circumscribed, and prostrate in adoration before the divine throne, to be made, and thus prostrate to overshadow the mercy-seat. It was fitting that the image of the heavenly choirs should overshadow the divine mysteries. Would you say that the Ark and staff and mercy-seat were not made? Are they not produced by the hand of man? Are they not due to what you call contemptible matter? What was the tabernacle itself? Was it not an image? Was it not a type and a figure? Hence the holy Apostle's words concerning the observances of the law, "Who serve unto the example and shadow, of heavenly things." As it was answered to Moses, when he was to finish the tabernacle: "See" (He says), "that thou make all things according to the pattern which was shown thee on the Mount." (Heb. 8.5; Ex. 25.40) But the law was not an image. It shrouded the image. In the words of the same Apostle, "the law contains the shadow of the goods to come, not the image of those things." (Heb. 10.1) For if the law should forbid images, and yet be itself a forerunner of images, what should we say? If the tabernacle was a figure, and the type of a type, why does the law not prohibit image-making? But this is not in the least the case. There is a time for everything. (Ecclesiastes 3:1)

Of old, God the incorporeal and uncircumscribed was never depicted. Now, however, when God is seen clothed in flesh, and conversing with men, (Baruch 3:38) I make an image of the God whom I see. I do not worship matter. I worship the God of matter, who became matter for my sake, and deigned to inhabit matter, who worked out my salvation through matter. I will not cease from honouring that matter which works my salvation. I venerate it, though not as God. How could God be born out of lifeless things? And if God's body is God by union, it is immutable.

The nature of God remains the same as before, the flesh created in time is quickened by a logical and reasoning soul. I honour all matter besides, and venerate it. Through it, filled, as it were, with a divine power and grace, my salvation has come to me. Was not the thrice happy and thrice blessed wood of the Cross matter? Was not the sacred and holy mountain of Calvary matter? What of the life-giving rock, the Holy Sepulchre, the source of our Resurrection: was it not matter? Is not the most holy book of the Gospels matter? Is not the blessed table matter which gives us the Bread of Life? Are not the gold and silver matter, out of which crosses and altar-plate and chalices are made? And before all these things, is not the body and blood of our Lord matter? Either do away with the veneration and worship due to all these things, or submit to the tradition of the Church in the worship of images, honouring God and His friends, and following in this the grace of the Holy Spirit. Do not despise matter, for it is not despicable. Nothing is that which God has made. This is the Manichean heresy. That alone is despicable which does not come from God, but is our own invention, the spontaneous choice of will to disregard the natural law – that is to say, sin.

If, therefore, you dishonour and give up images, because they are produced by matter, consider what the Scripture says: And the Lord spoke to Moses, saying, "Behold I have called by name Beseleel, the son of Uri, the son of Hur, of the tribe of Judah. And I have filled him with the spirit of God, with wisdom and understanding, and knowledge in all manner of work. To devise whatsoever may be artificially made of gold, and silver, and brass, of marble and precious stones, and variety of wood. And I have given him for his companion, Ooliab, the son of Achisamech, of the tribe of Dan. And I have put wisdom in the heart of every skilful man, that they may make all things which I have commanded thee." (Ex. 31:1-6) And again: "Moses said to all the assembly of the children of Israel: This is the word the Lord hath commanded, saying: Set aside with you first fruits to the Lord. Let everyone that is willing and hath a ready heart, offer them to the Lord, gold, and silver, and brass, violet, and purple, and scarlet twice dyed, and fine linen, goat's hair, and ram's skins died red and violet, coloured skins, selim-wood, and oil to maintain lights and to make ointment, and most sweet incense, onyx stones, and precious stones for the adorning of the ephod and the rational [Jewish High Priest's breastplate or 'rational' of judgement worn above the ephod. [See Catholic Encyclopedia, 1913] Whosoever of you is wise, let him come, and make that which the Lord hath commanded." (Ex. 35:4-10)

See you here the glorification of matter which you make inglorious. What is more insignificant than goat's hair or colours? Are not scarlet and purple and hyacinth colours? Now, consider the handiwork of man becoming the likeness of the cherubim. How, then, can you make the law a pretence for giving up what it orders? If you invoke it against images, you should keep the Sabbath, and practise circumcision. It is certain that "if you observe the law, Christ will not profit you. You who are justified in the law, you are fallen from grace." (St Paul's Letter to the Galatians 5:2-4) Israel of old did not see God, but "we see the Lord's glory face to face." (St Paul's Second Letter to the Corinthians 3:18) We proclaim Him also by our senses on all sides, and we sanctify the noblest sense, which is that of sight. The image is a memorial, just what words are to a listening ear. What a book is to the literate, that an image is to the illiterate. The image speaks to the sight as words to the ear; it brings us understanding.

Hence God ordered the Ark [of the Covenant] to be made of imperishable wood, and to be gilded outside and in, and the tablets to be put in it, and the staff and the golden urn containing the manna, for a remembrance of the past and a type of the future. Who can say these were not images and far-sounding heralds? And they did not hang on the walls of the tabernacle [of the Temple in Jerusalem]; but in sight of all the people who looked towards them, they were brought forward for the worship and adoration of God, who made use of them. It is evident that they were not worshipped for themselves, but that the people were led through them to remember past signs, and to worship the God of wonders. They were images to serve as recollections, not divine, but leading to divine things by Divine power. And God ordered twelve stones to be taken out of the Jordan, and specified why. For he says: "When your son asks you the meaning of these stones, tell him how the water left the Jordan by the divine command, and how the ark was saved and the whole people." (Joshua 4:21-22)

How, then, shall we not record on image the saving pains and wonders of Christ our Lord, so that when my child asks me, "What is this?" I may say, that God the Word became man, and that for His sake not Israel alone passed through the Jordan, but all the human race gained their original happiness. Through Him human nature rose from the lowest depths of the earth higher than the skies, and in His Person sat down on the throne His Father had prepared for Him.

But the adversary says: "Make an image of Christ or of His mother who bore Him and let that be sufficient." O what folly this is! On your own showing, you are absolutely against the saints. For if you make an image of Christ and not of the saints, it is evident that you do not disown images, but the honour of the saints. You make statues indeed of Christ as of one glorified, whilst you reject the saints as unworthy of honour, and call truth a falsehood. "I live," says the Lord, "and I will glorify those who glorify Me." (I Samuel 2:30) And the divine Apostle: therefore, now he is not a servant, but a son. "And if a son, an heir also through God." (Gal. 4.7) Again, "If we suffer with Him, that we also may be glorified:" (Rom. 8.17). You are not waging war against images, but against the saints. St John, who rested on His breast, says, that "we shall be like to Him" (First Letter of St John 3:2): just as a man by contact with fire becomes fire, not by nature, but by contact and by burning and by participation, so is it, I apprehend, with the flesh of the Crucified Son of God. That flesh, by participation through union with the Divine nature, was unchangeably God, not in virtue of grace from God as was the case with each of the prophets, but by the presence of the Fountain Head Himself. God, the Scripture says, stood in the synagogue of the gods, (Ps.82.1) so that the saints, too, are gods. Holy Gregory takes the words, "God stands in the midst of the gods," [Psalm 82:1] to mean that He discriminates their several merits. The saints in their lifetime were filled with the Holy Spirit, and when they are no more, His grace abides with their spirits and with their bodies in their tombs, and also with their likenesses and holy images, not by nature, but by grace and Divine power.

God charged David to build Him a temple through his son, and to prepare a place of rest. Solomon, in building the temple, made the cherubim, as the book of Kings says. And he encompassed the cherubim with gold, and all the walls in a circle, and he had the cherubim carved, and palms inside and out, in a circle, not from the sides, be it observed. And there were bulls and lions and pomegranates. (The First Book of Kings 6:28-29) Is it not more seemly to decorate all the walls of the Lord's house with holy forms and images rather than with beasts and plants?

Where is the law declaring "thou shalt not make any graven image"? But Solomon receiving the gift of wisdom, imaging Heaven, made the cherubim, and the likenesses of bulls and lions, which the law forbade. Now if we make a statue of Christ, and likenesses of the saints, does not their being filled with the Holy Ghost increase the piety of our homage? As then the people and the Temple were purified in blood and in burnt offerings, (Heb. 9:13) so now the Blood of Christ giving testimony under Pontius Pilate, (St Paul's First Letter to Timothy 6:13) and being Himself the first fruits of the martyrs, the Church is built up on the blood of the saints. Then the signs and forms of lifeless animals figured forth the human tabernacle, the martyrs themselves whom they were preparing for God's abode.

We depict Christ as our King and Lord, and do not deprive Him of His army. The saints constitute the Lord's army. Let the earthly king dismiss his army before he gives up his King and Lord. Let him put off the purple before he takes honour away from his most valiant men who have conquered their passions. For if the saints are heirs of God, and co-heirs of Christ, (Rom. 8:17) they will be also partakers of the Divine glory of sovereignty. If the friends of God have had a part in the sufferings of Christ, how shall they not receive a share of His glory even on earth? "I call you not servants," our Lord says, "you are my friends." (John 15:15)

Should we then deprive them of the honour given to them by the Church? What audacity! What boldness of mind, to fight God and His commands! You, who refuse to worship images, would not worship the Son of God, the Living Image of the invisible God, (Colossians 1:15) and His unchanging form. I worship the image of Christ as the Incarnate God; that of Our Lady, the Mother of us all, as the Mother of God's Son; that of the saints as the friends of God. They have withstood sin unto blood, and followed Christ in shedding their blood for Him, who shed His blood for them. I put on record the excellencies and the sufferings of those who have walked in His footsteps, that I may sanctify myself, and be fired with the zeal of imitation.

St Basil says, "Honouring the image leads to the prototype." If you raise churches to the saints of God, raise also their trophies. The Temple of old was not built in the name of any man. The death of the just was a cause of tears, not of feasting. A man who touched a corpse was considered unclean, (Numbers 19:11) even if the corpse was Moses himself. But now the memories of the saints are kept with rejoicings. The dead body of Jacob was wept over, whilst there is joy over the death of Stephen. Therefore, either give up the solemn commemorations of the saints, which are not according to the old law, or accept images which are also against it, as you say. But it is impossible not to keep with rejoicing the memories of the saints. The Holy Apostles and Fathers are at one in enjoining them.

From the time that God the Word became flesh He is as we are in everything except sin, and of our nature, without confusion. He has deified our flesh for ever, and we are in very deed sanctified through His Godhead and the union of His flesh with it. And from the time that God, the Son of God, impassable by reason of His Godhead, chose to suffer voluntarily He wiped out our debt, also paying for us a most full and noble ransom. We are truly free through the Sacred Blood of the Son pleading for us with the Father. And we are indeed delivered from corruption since He descended into hell to the souls detained there through centuries (First Letter of St Peter 3:19) and gave the captives their freedom, sight to the blind, (Matthew 12:29) and chaining the strong one. He rose in the plenitude of His power, keeping the flesh of immortality which He had taken for us. And since we have been born again of water and the Spirit, we are truly sons and heirs of God. Hence St Paul calls the faithful holy; (I Corinthians 1:2) hence we do not grieve but rejoice over the death of the saints. We are then no longer under grace, (Rom. 6:14) being justified through faith, (Rom. 5:1) and knowing the one true God. The just man is not bound by the law. (I. Tim. 1:9) We are not held by the letter of the Law, nor do we serve as children, (Galatians 4:1) but grown into the perfect estate of man we are fed on solid food, not on that which conduces to idolatry.

The Law is good as a light shining in a dark place until the day breaks. Your hearts have already been illuminated, the living water of God's knowledge has run over the tempestuous seas of heathendom, and we may all know God. The old creation has passed away, and all things are renovated. The holy Apostle Paul said to St Peter, the chief of the Apostles: "If you, being a Jew, live as a heathen and not a Jew, how will you persuade heathens to do as Jews do?" (Gal. 2:14) And to the Galatians: "I will bear witness to every circumcised man that it is salutary to fulfil the whole law." (Gal. 5:3)

Of old they who did not know God, worshipped false gods. But now, knowing God, or rather being known by Him, how can we return to bare and naked rudiments? (Gal. 4:8-9) I have looked upon the human form of God, and my soul has been saved. I gaze upon the image of God, as Jacob did, (Genesis 32:30) though in a different way. Jacob sounded the note of the future, seeing with immaterial sight, whilst the image of Him who is visible to flesh is burnt into my soul. The shadow and winding sheet and relics of the Apostles cured sickness, and put demons to flight. (Acts 5:15) How, then, shall not the shadow and the statues of the saints be glorified? Either do away with the worship of all matter, or be not an innovator.

Do not disturb the boundaries of centuries, put up by your fathers. (Proverbs 22:28) It is not in writing only that they have bequeathed to us the tradition of the Church, but also in certain unwritten examples. In the twenty-seventh book of his work, in thirty chapters addressed to Amphilochios concerning the Holy Spirit, St Basil says, "In the cherished teaching and dogmas of the Church, we hold some things by written documents; others we have received in mystery from the Apostolical tradition." Both are of equal value for the soul's growth. No one will dispute this who has considered even a little the discipline of the Church. For if we neglect unwritten customs as not having much weight, we bury in oblivion the most pertinent facts connected with the Gospel. These are the great Basil's words. How do we know the Holy place of Calvary, or the Holy Sepulchre? Does it not rest on a tradition handed down from father to son? It is written that our Lord was crucified on Calvary, and buried in a tomb, which Joseph hewed out of the rock (Matthew 27:60); but it is unwritten tradition which identifies these spots, and does more things of the same kind. Whence come the three immersions at Baptism, praying with face turned towards the east, and the tradition of the mysteries? Hence St Paul says, "Therefore, brethren, stand fast, and hold the traditions which you have learned either by word, or by our epistle." (Second Letter to the Thessalonians 2:15)

As, then, so much has been handed down in the Church, and is observed down to the present day, why disparage images? If you bring forward certain practices, they do not inculpate our worship of images, but the worship of heathens who make them idols. Because heathens do it foolishly, this is no reason for objecting to our pious practice. If the same magicians and sorcerers use supplication, so does the Church with catechumens; the former invoke devils, but the Church calls upon God against devils. Heathens have raised up images to demons, whom they call gods. Now we have raised them to the one Incarnate God, to His servants and friends, who are proof against the diabolical hosts.

If, again, you object that the great Epiphanius thoroughly rejected images, I would say in the first place the work in question is fictitious and unauthentic. It bears the name of someone who did not write it, which used to be commonly done. Secondly, we know that blessed Athanasius objected to the bodies of saints being put into chests, and that he preferred their burial in the ground, wishing to set at nought the strange custom of the Egyptians, who did not bury their dead underground, but set them upon beds and couches. Thus, supposing that he really wrote this work, the great Epiphanius, wishing to correct something of the same kind, ordered that images should not be used. The proof that he did not object to images, is to be found in his own church, which is adorned with images to this day. Thirdly, the exception is not a law to the Church, neither does one swallow make summer, as it seems to Gregory the theologian, and to the truth. Neither can one expression overturn the tradition of the whole Church which is spread throughout the world.

Accept, therefore, the teaching of Scripture and spiritual writers. If the Scripture does call "the idols of heathens silver and gold, and the works of man's hand," (Psalm 135:15) it does not forbid the adoration of inanimate things, or man's handiwork, but the adoration of demons.

We have seen that prophets worshipped angels, and men, and kings, and the impious, and even a staff. David says, "And you adore His footstool." (Psalm 99:5) Isaias, speaking in God's name, says, "The heavens are my throne, and the earth my footstool." (Isaiah 66:1) Now, it is evident to everyone that the heavens and the earth are created things. Moses, too, and Aaron with all the people, adored the work of hands. St Paul, the golden grasshopper of the Church, says in his Epistle to the Hebrews, "But Christ being come, a high priest of the good things to come, by a greater and more perfect tabernacle not made by hand," that is "not of this creation." And, again, "For Jesus is not entered into the Holies made by hands, the patterns of the true; but into Heaven itself." (Heb. 9:11, 24) Thus the former holy things, the tabernacle, and everything within it, were made by hands, and no one denies that they were adored.

REFLECTIONS

"Life is an opportunity, benefit from it.
Life is beauty, admire it. Life is a dream, realize it.
Life is a challenge, meet it.
Life is a duty, complete it. Life is a game, play it.
Life is a promise, fulfil it. Life is sorrow, overcome it.
Life is a song, sing it. Life is a struggle, accept it.
Life is a tragedy, confront it. Life is an adventure, dare it.
Life is luck, make it. Life is too precious, do not destroy it.
Life is life, fight for it."

❦ St Mother Teresa of Calcutta

"The good you do today may be forgotten tomorrow.
Do good anyway. Give the world the best you have
and it may never be enough. Give your best anyway.
For you see, in the end, it is between you and God.
It was never between you and them anyway."

❦ St Mother Teresa of Calcutta

"The final battle between the Lord and the
kingdom of Satan will be about
Marriage and the Family."

❦ Sr Lucia of Fatima

"As the family goes, so goes the nation and
so goes the whole world in which we live."

❦ St John Paul II

It's as if your guardian Angel were saying to you:
"You fill your heart with so much human attachment! . . .
And that, then, is what you want your Guardian to guard!"

≫ St Josemaria Escriva

Dear Lord, Thou knowest my weakness. Each morning
I resolve to be humble, and in the evening I recognize
that I have often been guilty of pride. The sight of these
faults tempts me to discouragement; yet I know that
discouragement is itself but a form of pride. I wish, therefore,
O my God, to build all my trust upon Thee. As Thou canst
do all things, deign to implant in my soul this virtue which
I desire, and to obtain it from Thy Infinite Mercy, I will often
say to Thee: "Jesus, Meek and Humble of Heart,
make my heart like unto Thine."

≫ St Thérèse of Lisieux

"Let nothing disturb you, let nothing frighten you, all things
are passing away: God never changes. Patience obtains all
things Whoever has God lacks nothing; God alone suffices."

≫ St Teresa of Avila

"It is true that our dispositions do not cause the grace of the
sacrament: all they do is to give it free course, by removing
the obstacles: but we must open our hearts as widely as
possible to the outpouring of the Divine Gift. An excellent
disposition then, is to try to refuse nothing to Christ.
A soul that remains habitually in this disposition of putting
away all that could offend the sight of the Divine Guest, and
holding itself ready to accomplish His Divine Will,
is admirably "adapted" for the Sacramental action."

≫ Blessed Columba Marmion, *Christ the Life of the Soul*

"Do not seek to have your trials removed,
ask rather for the grace to bear them well."

🌿 St Andre Bassette

"To doubt is the greatest insult to the Divinity"

🌿 Padre Pio

"To repent is not to look downwards at my own
shortcomings, but upwards at God's love; it is not to look
backwards with self-reproach but forward with trustfulness,
it is not to see what I have failed to be, but what by the grace
of God I might yet become."

🌿 St John Climacus

"Indeed, it is now clear that the soul of a faithful person,
the most worthy of all creatures because of the grace of God,
is greater that heaven itself, since the heavens and the
rest of creation cannot contain their creator;
only a faithful person is His dwelling place and throne…"

🌿 St Clare of Assisi

"Of all the demons, the one that most holds
men back and prevents them from being happy is
"what could have been and was not."
The past is left to the mercy of God and
the future to His providence.
Only the present is in our hands.
Live today loving God with all your heart."

🌿 St Alphonsus Liguori

NOTES

The Rosary

St Louis de Montfort (1673-1716) says Mary told St Dominic (1170-1221) that when God planned to renew the face of the earth He started by sending down rain from Heaven, and this was the angel Gabriel's salutation to Mary. King David alludes to this salutation when he proclaimed, "I will sing a new song to you." This song still waters the earth in the form of a prayer called the Rosary.

"If anyone thirsts, let him come to Me."
(JOHN 7:37)

St Catherine of Sienna was given to understand that, "If anyone thirsts," means to thirst for virtue, God's honour and the salvation of souls. The heart being the vessel which carries the water and the heart is perfected when there is unity of will, intellect and memory, all centerer on God, because only then can the soul sustain a thirst that leads to the fulfillment of the commandments; namely, "to love God above everything, and your neighbour as yourself." (*The Dialogue*, Tan Classics, Pgs. 74-76)

Tradition: Word of Mouth and in Writing

In his Apologia (The Defence of Icons) the Damascene recalls how St Basil (330-379) defends the Apostolic tradition:

"Do not disturb the boundaries of centuries, put up by your fathers. (Proverbs 22:28) It is not in writing only that they have bequeathed to us the tradition of the Church, but also in certain unwritten examples. In the twenty-seventh book of his work, in thirty chapters addressed to Amphilochios concerning the Holy Spirit, St Basil says, 'In the cherished teaching and dogmas of the Church, we hold some things by written documents; others we have received in mystery from the Apostolical tradition.' Both are of equal value for the soul's growth."

Suicide

(2280) Everyone is responsible for his life before God who has given it to him. It is God who remains the sovereign Master of life. We are obliged to accept life gratefully and preserve it for his honour and the salvation of our souls. We are stewards, not owners, of the life God has entrusted to us. It is not ours to dispose of.

(2281) Suicide contradicts the natural inclination of the human being to preserve and perpetuate his life. It is gravely contrary to the just love of self. It likewise offends love of neighbour because it unjustly breaks the ties of solidarity with family, nation, and other human societies to which we continue to have obligations. Suicide is contrary to love for the living God.

(2282) If suicide is committed with the intention of setting an example [e.g. Suicide bombers], especially to the young, it also takes on the gravity of scandal. Voluntary co-operation in suicide is contrary to the moral law.

> Grave psychological disturbances, anguish, or grave fear of hardship, suffering, or torture can diminish the responsibility of the one committing suicide.

(2283) We should not despair of the eternal salvation of persons who have taken their own lives. By ways known to him alone, God can provide the opportunity for salutary repentance. The Church prays for persons who have taken their own lives.

❦ CATECHISM OF THE CATHOLIC CHURCH

PICTURES

Cover	Rainbow over Meteora, Greece. Photo by Keiron Long
Page 22	Former Cathedral of St. Sophia, Istanbul (Constantinople) / Wikimedia Commons
Page 86	Otranto Cathedral. Photo by Keiron Long
Page 90	Konstantinos Kanaris. Collection of Greek Parliament / Wikimedia Commons.
Page 101	Miracle of the Sun / Wikimedia Commons.
Page 108	Our Lady of Guadalupe Mexico, 1531 / Wikimedia Commons.
Back Cover	The Bones of the Otranto martyrs in a side chapel of Otranto Cathedral. Photo by Keiron Long.

MAPS

Page 9	Arabia in the time of Muhammed / Wikimedia Commons.
Page 15	Byzantine and Sassanid Empires in 600 AD / Wikimedia Commons.

REFERENCES

The Holy Quran: Translations and Commentaries. 2nd ed. Istanbul: n.p., 2003. (ISBN 975-96011-2-5.)

Thomas Aquinas. *Summa Theologica*: A Concise Translation. Edited by Timothy McDermott. Notre Dame, IN: Ave Maria Press, 1989. Paperback ed., 1991.

Donner, Fred M. *Muhammad and the Believers: At the Origins of Islam*. Cambridge, MA: Harvard University Press, 2012.

McAuliffe, Jane Dammen, ed. *The Cambridge Companion to the Qur'an*. Cambridge: Cambridge University Press, 2006.

Ohlig, Karl-Heinz, and Gerd-R. Puin, eds. *The Hidden Origins of Islam*. Amherst, NY: Prometheus Books, 2010.

Holland, T. *In the Shadow of the Sword*. Little Brown, 2002.

www.academia.edu

BIBLIOGRAPHY

1. Crone, P. Slaves on Horseback. Cambridge: Cambridge University Press, 1980. Paperback edition, 2003, p. 25.
2. Spoerl, J. "Muhammad and the Jews according to Ibn Ishaq." Levantine Review 2, no. 1 (Spring 2013).
3. Hitti, P. K. History of the Arabs: From the Earliest Times to the Present. London: Macmillan, 1970. 10th ed., p. 143.
4. Ibid., p. 147.
5. Hoyland, R. G. In God's Path: The Arab Conquests and the Creation of an Islamic Empire. Oxford: Oxford University Press, 2015. Paperback, 2017, p. 95.
6. Hitti, p. 142–43.
7. Pipes, D. "The Muslim Claim to Jerusalem." Middle East Quarterly 8, no. 4 (Fall 2001): 35–45.

8. Ibid., p. 40
9. Hitti, p. 221.
10. Azhari Andi and Hamdi Putra Ahmed. "Before Orthodoxy: The Story of Abraham's Sacrifice (Dzabih) in Early Muslim Commentaries." International Journal of Islamic Khazanah (https://journal.uinsgd.ac.id/index.php/ijik).
11. Saint John of Damascus. The Fount of Knowledge, Part 2: Heresies, ch. 101.
12. Von Balthasar, H. U., ed. The Scandal of the Incarnation: Irenaeus Against the Heresies. San Francisco: Ignatius Press, 1990, p. 74.
13. Hughes, P. A History of the Church, Vol. 1. New York: Sheed & Ward, 1949, p. 241.
14. Tacitus. Annals, Book 15.
15. The Catechism of the Catholic Church. Homebush, NSW: St Pauls, 1994, p. 347.
16. Ibid., p. 344.
17. Von Balthasar, p. 83.
18. Ibid., p. 83.
19. Algar, Thorold, ed. The Dialogue of St. Catherine of Siena. USA: TAN Classics, 2010, p. 49.
20. John, Bishop of Nikiou. Chronicle, ch. 110 (CX).
21. Hitti, p. 164.
22. Fernandez-Morera, D. The Myth of the Andalusian Paradise: Muslims, Christians, and Jews under Islamic Rule in Medieval Spain. Wilmington, DE: ISI Books, 2016, p. 121–122.
23. Isidore of Beja. Chronicle of 754.
24. Hitti, p. 602.
25. Hitti, p. 315.
26. Einhard. The Life of Charlemagne, ch. 25.
27. Von Balthasar, pp. 19–20.
28. Stark, R. Bearing False Witness: Debunking Centuries of Anti-Catholic History. West Conshohocken, PA: Templeton Press, 2016, p. 205.

www.ingramcontent.com/pod-product-compliance
Lightning Source LLC
Chambersburg PA
CBHW061442040426
42450CB00007B/1176